D1024833

How to Think
Like a Winner

James C. Lewis

UNITY BOOKS
Unity Village, Missouri

CONTENTS

How to Think
Like a Winner

Everyone would like to be a winner. Everyone can be a winner. However, before we can win at anything we must ask ourselves: Am I willing to do what a winner must do? Am I willing to entertain and accept the challenging thoughts necessary to be a winner? Many people want the status, the praise, the rewards, and the feeling of self-esteem a winner experiences, but they do not want to do the hard thinking or hard work necessary to win.

When we consider from a negative human viewpoint the type of thinking that is necessary to win, it may at first seem difficult. However, when we accept the challenge, we find it is actually more difficult to think like a loser. A winner's thoughts guarantee success, happiness, and achievement; a loser's thoughts guarantee misery, dejection, failure, and poverty. A winner's success may take a long time to come. But success never comes for a loser.

I would like to share with you five winning ideas, any one of which will bring improvement. We should see ourselves ultimately thinking and expressing all five, having incorporated them into our unconscious thought processes. This is not a comprehensive list by any means, but it will open the door for other thoughts and ideas to be revealed. These ideas are not necessarily in order, for the order is determined by the need of our consciousness and the circumstances of our lives.

First: A definite objective. A winner has a definite major objective in his life. He knows where he should go, and he desires to go there. A loser is always wondering what he should be doing with his life. He cannot decide, for he has no definite objective to guide him in making decisions. A winner, knowing where he is going, finds it easier to make decisions. He knows what to eliminate from his thoughts and life. A loser is always putting off and affirming he will get started tomorrow. A winner is decisive because he knows where he wants to go, and even more important he knows he should go there. Without an objective we are tossed about on the waves of life's experiences and seem to get nowhere. With an objective our lives are stable; we have a definite port toward which we are traveling and, provided the other necessary ingredients are added, we will get to that port.

Second: Determination. This is sometimes referred to as the "will to succeed." Jesus expressed it this way, *"Not my will, but thine, be done."* Jesus knew what His objective was, and He was determined to carry it out no matter how difficult. He knew it was a divine objective. The winner does not let failure keep him down. Even when it seems there is no way to win, he keeps going and trying; he never gives up. The loser is constantly looking for an excuse to give up, always thinking of what is against him. The winner, because of his determination, is always thinking about what is for him and is seeking a way to win. If we do not have determination, we will not stick, and if we do not stick, we will not win. Determination is the ability to hold tight while growth is taking place inside and around us. Determination is motivation to win.

Third: A strong belief in self. Instead of putting himself down, thinking others' thoughts about him, a winner puts himself up, not in an egotistical way but in a reassuring, confident way. A winner does not need constant praise or approval from others. He does not need their reassurance. He believes in himself, the God-self within him. Believing in the spiritual self is believing in the "Father within," to whom Jesus referred so often and in whom He said we should believe. The winner knows his value even if others do not. He does not wait until others accept his ideas or are ready to go along with him on his goals. He knows his own acceptance is more important. Because of his healthy thinking about himself, he has absolute confidence. He has the courage to step out and win. The winner does not need the false security of past successes to bolster a shaky ego. His success may be built upon past failures from which he has learned. Therefore, in his thinking they were not failures; they were learning experiences. A winner does not have a stranglehold on things or people, for he is free and respects the freedom of others. He has a contagious self-confidence that attracts others to help him in achieving his goals; and by attracting these people, he is indirectly helping them achieve their goals.

Fourth: A willingness to work while others play. Most people spend much of their time thinking about how they can be entertained during their non-working hours. Even while they are supposed to be working, they are often thinking about what they can do later.

7

This is why the phrase TGIF ("Thank God It's Friday") is so popular. Before you misunderstand me, let me say that I believe one should have times for recreation and renewal. However, to reach a goal one must be willing to work unhampered by the distraction of plans for future escapades of self-indulgence. The winner knows that one day he can choose his own working hours. Because of his willingness to work, a winner does not complain about the tasks to be done. He does not classify things to be done as hard or easy, or clean or dirty. He does what has to be done. He realizes that along the pathway toward success there will be many varied experiences, some more challenging than others maybe, but he doesn't shirk from the difficult ones; he just gets them done. A winner is not a seeker of the limelight; he seeks to serve, and this often puts him in the limelight. A winner does not just think about the money he will make for himself, he thinks more about the service he will give to others. His joy is in giving. A winner always seeks to do more than he is "paid" for, knowing the law of compensation will take care of him. He can discipline himself and sacrifice immediate pleasures and gains, if need be, for a greater goal or purpose.

Fifth: A winner is a positive and constructive thinker. A loser is a negative thinker who is certain nothing works for him. A winner marshals his thoughts and feelings behind constructive ideas and goals. His mind is alert to thoughts of achievement. He does not dwell on destructive thoughts. A winner gives his mind to the constructive side of life, even in meeting negative challenges. A winner knows that the only way to master a situation is to master his thoughts about that situation, and he values ideas and thinking about ideas more than he values things. He knows that thoughts will get him things, but things will not always get him the ideas and thoughts he needs to win. A winner knows that right thinking will enable him to rise above even physical limitations.

The more we think like a winner the easier it becomes to win. If we think like a loser, life becomes more difficult. It is more enjoyable to win. It is more profitable to win. It is more rewarding to win. And we can all win if we want to!

A Prerequisite for Winning

The subject of this chapter is so vital that much of our positive thinking and effort can be negated if this area is neglected. We may make progress for a while without giving it any consideration, but we will one day have to take it into account if we want to be total winners.

What is this vital subject? It can be stated in one word: *forgiveness*. It does not take much observation to realize that the world if filled with hate. This hate is destructive to the attainment of world peace as well as individual peace. Some of this hate is expressed as "righteous indignation." There are people who think they have a right to hate those who have wronged them and caused them to suffer. They *do* have this right; but, if they exercise it, they will have to accept the consequences. Those consequences will never be sweet, for revenge is bitter. This is true even if a person seems to get material benefits from his revenge.

When a person is filled with hate and the desire for revenge, he seeks to destroy others. He does not realize this Truth: *He who hates destroys himself.* He destroys his peace of mind first of all, and if he persists he will eventually destroy his health. There are other negative consequences, but we will not go into them here. Our interest is in dealing with this subject on a positive level.

Forgiveness is essential to winning at the game of life. Forgiveness is the ability to express love under adverse conditions. It is the ability to respond to negative actions of others with love and understanding. It is the ability to give love in return for some destructive remark or criticism. It is the ability to release harmful emotions and replace them with constructive, loving ones.

Thoughts and feelings of criticism, condemnation, resentment, vengefulness, hatred, or refusal to cooperate block the expression of the dynamic winning qualities of love, faith, power, and enthusiasm, which are essential to successful living.

Jesus recognized the destructive power of hate, and that is why He suggested that we forgive those who take advantage of us and use us for their personal gain. Hating someone for what is lost will never restore that loss. Love is the great restoring power. Love is the power that rebuilds and replenishes what seems to have been lost. The restoration may not be of the same personality or the identical object, but love fills the void; and when that happens we see things with a fresh, new perspective. We don't see and dwell on what someone has done to us; we dwell instead on the love and good we can do for them.

When we get upset, disturbed, or even furious at someone, it is a sign that we need to check up on ourselves, not the other person. It is not a time to dwell on what he is doing wrong; it is a time to get a true perspective about him, a time to seek to understand him and to express love toward him.

12

Instead of trying to get rid of a person, we need to get rid of the negative thoughts we have about that person; we need to release the negative emotions we are experiencing.

Trying to find peace of mind by running away from a distasteful person or situation is a waste of time, for we shall confront another such person—if not the same one—somewhere else. Forgiveness enables us to set things straight in our consciousness so we can avoid these negative attractions.

I have known individuals who have harbored deep-seated resentments toward members of their own families for more than twenty years. What a price to pay for cherished resentments! These people probably never realized the connection between their resentments and their health.

If you are wondering about the effect of anger on your health, let me tell you of this experience a friend of mine had many years ago. He told me that one day on his way home from work he stopped at a neighborhood gas station to fill the car's tank. He had stopped there many times and knew the attendant fairly well. In the course of their conversation, something was said that made my friend angry. By the time he got home he had begun to lose the ability to speak. The next day he visited a doctor, and he was quite surprised at what he was told. He had been expecting the doctor to say he was coming down with a cold. Instead, the doctor said, "All you have to do is forgive someone."

In our culture we are taught through implication that one who practices nonresistance and forgiveness becomes a "doormat" and others will take advantage of and walk on him. These are mistaken concepts. A person who demands retribution through hate and resentment becomes more than a doormat; he becomes a slave. He becomes enslaved to negative and bitter thoughts and feelings that make his life miserable and, if persisted in, will make him sick. He cannot control his thoughts, feelings, attitudes, or even his behavior. Some people under the influence of these negative emotions have spontaneously done things that have resulted in jail sentences. The person with love in his heart gains; the one with hate loses.

Here is another way to look at it: When a negative thought about another person can arouse bitter feelings in us, that person has power over us. We have given him the power to make us feel miserable, perhaps even the power to cause us to do things we will later regret.

When a person is debating whether or not to forgive, this or a similar thought may arise: He does not deserve to be forgiven. Included in *forgiveness* is the idea of giving love to a person whom or situation that, according to human values and thinking, may not deserve it. It is not a matter of deserving (though all persons are) but a matter of need. Forgiveness is needed in order to bring peace, harmony, freedom, and right relationships.

One of the most important things we can develop in life is a forgiving consciousness. This is an unconscious response of forgiveness to every difficult person we encounter and every unpleasant situation we become involved in. This is something we will want to work at every day. We will need to confront some of our negative responses and make a conscious effort to

14

forgive. An affirmative prayer to help us do this is: *I now forgive all who have ever offended me, and I ask forgiveness of all whom I have offended. I do so without any reservations or conditions.*

Has someone hurt you through criticism? Forgive him. Has someone cheated you? Forgive him. Has someone taken advantage of you? Forgive him. Has someone made your life miserable? Forgive him. Are you thinking this is too hard to do? Remember, it is a hundred times more difficult to carry around bitterness and grudges. Even if a person gets the so-called human satisfaction of seeking and getting revenge, he loses. There is no way we can win happiness, peace, health, prosperity, or success through hate; and that is why a true winner overcomes this negative emotion. If he has any tendency whatsoever along this line, he immediately seeks to transform that emotion into one of love.

In our normal human way of thinking we may have had the tendency to say, "I will gladly forgive if. . . . " That is toleration, not forgiveness. The more noble and winning way is to say, "I will forgive regardless." This means that we will forgive regardless of whether or not the other person apologizes or makes amends.

The experience of releasing bitter memories and resentment may not be easy, but it is a prerequisite to winning in this wonderful adventure of life.

Goal-Setting

Do you have any idea where you will be or what you will be doing five or ten years from now? You may think there are too many variables to be precise about your future. You may think there are too many uncertainties; too much fate or chance to deal with; too many unknowables. Your future does not have to be left to these unknowables. You can determine where you will be and what you will be doing. It is up to you to decide what type of life you want to experience.

We go where we dream about. We go where our thoughts take us. If we think about unpleasant things, ten years from now we will be experiencing unpleasant things, unless we change our thinking. We are not pawns in the hands of a changing and unpredictable god. We can achieve any goal we set for ourselves as long as we accept the responsibility of making ourselves worthy channels to express the ideal. The power of accomplishment is within us waiting to be tapped and used.

Of course, our decisions may require that we learn to develop self-control in order to achieve our goals; but, if we will make this effort, we will have more confidence and a greater feeling of certainty about our futures than those who drift along in life with no purpose and a complete lack of direction.

If you are to have a happy, peaceful, and rewarding life, if you are to be the winner you want to be, then it is essential that you have goals to think about and to work toward achieving. Goals give meaning, direction, and purpose to our lives. The unhappy person is the one who feels life is beyond his power to control. He thinks he must just take what life has to offer him, and he does not think life has very much to offer that is worthwhile. So he goes his way, seeking various forms of sensory stimulation to keep himself from getting bored.

Then there are those who want to get somewhere in life but do not know where. They want to be happy, but they do not know what will make them happy. They want to be successful, but they do not know what to do to make themselves feel successful. These people are like ships on the ocean without rudders. They feel they have no power to control their courses nor to know their destinations. The fact is, they are not going anywhere.

It does not have to be that way for you. You can become the captain at the helm. God has given you a wonderful mind and unlimited potential of talent and ability to achieve a worthwhile, successful life. He has given you the power to think, feel, and visualize. By using these wonderful tools constructively, you can achieve your heart's desire; you can be what you sincerely want to be. When you can believe this with all your heart, nothing will prevent the achievement of your goals.

There are many books that deal with the subject of setting goals. Many of them are good, and what they say about achieving goals is practical. However, there is one serious shortcoming: They leave out a very important point, which, if heeded, will save you much frustration and anguish. I know, for I learned this lesson the difficult way. Fortunately, my experience did not turn out to be the disaster it could have been.

It began in 1953 when I read a book and became excited about the tremendous things I could do and have if I were only willing to work at it. The work was simple. The book instructed me to make a list of the things I wanted to do, and then add the things I wanted to have, such as money, clothes, an automobile, a home, and vacations. Of course, I was supposed to put on that list the service I was going to give so that I could make the money to pay for all these things. At the time I wanted to be a salesman, and I put that on my list.

After I had composed the list, I was supposed to read it each night before I went to bed; and this I did with strong feelings of anticipation and eagerness, looking forward to the moment when these things would begin to appear. But the results I began to get were not results I wanted. I woke up each night with a tremendous feeling of fear and apprehension. What happened? Well, in addition to the ritual I performed before going to bed, there was one I was practicing in the morning. At that time I would meditate and ask God to guide, direct, and show me what I should do to be successful. I assumed that what I wanted to do was the best plan to follow. It finally dawned on me that there was a serious conflict of purpose—my human plans did not mesh with the direction I was getting in my time of meditation. I tore up the list I had made and composed a new one based on the guidance received in meditation. This led me in a totally different direction, which I thought at first would not offer the opportunities of happiness and success I had planned to achieve. I was wrong!

The point is this: When you are setting goals, it is important that you be willing to let go of personal plans and become receptive to the super plan, the plan God will reveal to you. His goals for us are usually more challenging than the ones we set for ourselves; they are also more rewarding and fulfilling.

An affirmative prayer that can help you get in touch with divine purpose is this: *God in me is infinite wisdom; He shows me what to do and I am willing to accept it and do it.* As you affirm this, be willing to let go of any previous plan of what you thought was best for you. Be completely open and receptive to what He is ready and willing to reveal to you. Know that He wants to guide you in a way that you will find happy and rewarding. You do not have to be afraid that He will lead you to do something unpleasant, even though it may at first seem that way to you and to others.

When you seek this major purpose, you will discover that it is easy to set minor goals, for they will always be related to your major purpose. If you come up with something detrimental to your major purpose, you will know clearly and without doubt that it is not for you.

As you consider setting goals, you might find it helpful to think of both long-range and short-term goals. Long-range goals give the mind plenty to work on, something constructive to look forward to. Also, we experience the joy of expectation and accomplishment along the way. It may take special training or education to achieve our long-range goals. We may need to learn to be more understanding or nonresistant, or to think positively, or to stand firm in the face of trying and challenging times. If we want to be successful, we may need to learn our responsibility and how to accept it. We cannot go forward to something greater until we have learned some of the small things necessary to sustain us in our important goal. Before a soldier is sent into battle he is given specialized training. Before we send children out on their own we attempt to give them education and spiritual training. When we set long-range goals, we must be prepared to receive some training.

Short-term goals consist of those things we wish to accomplish soon. They are readily attainable goals. We need to have periodic accomplishments to keep from falling into negative thought that assumes we are not making progress. It is good to stretch our mental and emotional capacities, but be sure to have small successes along the way with short-term goals.

A runner prepares for a marathon. If he is starting from scratch, having done very little or no running, the marathon is a long-range goal, perhaps two years away. The runner's short-term goals will be to develop the ability to run five, then ten, then fifteen, then twenty miles, gradually building up strength and endurance.

We should also classify our long- and short-range goals into categories of "personal" and "impersonal." Personal goals are ones that focus on personal benefit. They might be for the improvement of consciousness and character, or the development of talents and abilities. One of them may be the goal of becoming free of some undesirable habit. Another may be setting up a regular regimen for the development of the mind through meditation, reading good books, and attending classes for the study of Truth principles.

Impersonal goals are the things you intend to do for others or for an organization to which you belong. These involve the giving of a portion of your time, talent, and money to support something that may not give you any direct personal benefit, except the joy of doing. They will be goals wherein you seek to give without any thought of getting something in return.

Misleading temptations often come in the form of offers of quick, easy, effortless success. They sometimes promise great rewards, giving illustrations of how winners have achieved fame and fortune. You may be told how easy it is for the winner to perform his feat, whether it is in sports, finance, or good health.

Yes, it is easy for a winner, for he is in condition to win. He has developed the attitudes of mind, heart, and body that enable him to do his task easily. When we hear Artur Rubinstein play the piano, it seems easy for him; and it is. When we hear of J. P. Morgan, who made fantastic sums of money, we think it is easy to make money; and it is, when one knows how. When we hear of someone who has good health, keeps his weight where it should be, and is physically fit, we say it is easy for him to be that way; and it is. It may not have been easy at first; but, once proper mental attitudes were developed and emotional and physical discipline were learned, then it was easy.

When we are thinking of setting goals for our lives, it is important that we do not set compromising goals. A true goal is something that captivates our interest

22

and enthusiasm. It is something we would really like to do and that we feel is worthwhile, important, and beneficial, not only to us but to others. If we think there are too many persons in that particular field already, we may compromise and seek other pastures. Or if we think what we want to do is too far beyond our ability and possibilities, we may tend to set a compromising and less demanding goal.

But we will never be satisfied with a compromise. We will always wonder what might have happened if we had followed our inner inclination, our true one rather than our human one. One small step toward a true goal is worth more than a hundred big strides toward a compromise. There are feelings of accomplishment and success in that one small step.

The human plan for goal achievement is very simple: Decide what you want; believe that you can get what you want; visualize what you want; and you will soon have it. This formula will work wonders in getting outer results. But it will not necessarily work to give us the inner results, such as happiness in our accomplishments, a feeling of self-esteem, a sense of worthy purpose in what we have done, and countless other wonderful feelings. Not all goal-achievers are happy and satisfied people; many of them are restless, dissatisfied, and unhappy.

The better formula for goal-setting is first to learn our divine direction. The next step is to believe that we can develop ourselves to the point of expressing this divine idea. Then we see ourselves accomplishing and fulfilling the divine plan. Next we do whatever we can at the moment to take the first small step in the outer toward the fulfillment of that plan. If we cannot

23

take a step, we simply stand and face that way until we can. If we will face the right direction, which simply means that we hold in our minds the thing we feel we should do, we will eventually overcome the human inertia, resistance, and doubt. We will become spiritually motivated. When this happens, we will begin to move and nothing will be able to stop us, for we will be moving with God, and God will be moving us. This is an unbeatable combination!

Out of this movement will come spiritual confidence and enthusiasm, like a perpetual flame that will keep you moving, both when it is rough going and easy going. A winner trains all the time—when it is easy and when it is difficult. Persistence is one of the characteristics in the cycle of progress.

It is a good idea to write down your goals in order to get them out of your head, where you may hash them over and never do anything with them. Write them on a card and carry it with you; read them over many times each day. Think about them; dream about them; visualize yourself achieving them. Doing this will help you to realize more fully what you really want to accomplish. You will no doubt cross some things off and add new goals in the form of affirmations and repeat them many times. Something I found beneficial years ago was to carry paper and pencils with me. When I found myself in a position where there was time going to waste, I would get out my pencil and paper and write affirmations. This impressed my subconscious mind. Constant presentation of your plans, goals, and true desires to the conscious and subconscious facets of your mind will help you develop the consciousness necessary eventually to achieve your meaningful goals.

As you make it a daily practice to seek the guidance of the creative intelligence within you, it will become a simple matter to make a spiritual goal list related to many areas of your life. Achieving these spiritual goals will make you the winner you want to be and were created to be.

Knowing the Best for You

When there is a need for guidance, it is reassuring to know there is a Source within you that is accurate, dependable, and available. Often, when we need an answer, we search in the world of appearances for someone or something to guide and direct us. We look for someone who is supposed to be an authority, or we look for signs or symbols that are supposed to be indications of what is best for us. Such outer seeking is never satisfying, for we are often left with the feeling of doubt or apprehension about the answers we have gotten. In outer seeking there is no feeling of certainty that we are following a path that will meet our need.

God within is our only absolutely reliable source of guidance. He knows us and our needs better than we know ourselves. He knows us better than anyone else ever will. He can lead us in a clear way that will give us a feeling of certainty, a knowing that we are following guidance that will help us rise above or victoriously meet our challenges.

The way of trying to get guidance from outer signs is fraught with problems and difficulties. For example, one may go to another person and attempt to give all the necessary information dealing with a personal problem and then ask for advice. However, even though a detailed explanation is given, it is impossible

27

to reveal to another all the factors necessary to make a divine decision, for many of them are unconscious. Only God's Spirit within each of us knows all that is necessary to guide us accurately.

This does not mean we should not talk with others about our problems. Sometimes it is helpful to talk with others, for it releases the negative thinking and feeling so that we may be open and receptive to inner guidance. In the final analysis, we must recognize our own inner feeling. We should never follow someone else's opinion without an inner verification. In our need for guidance, we must learn to wait for this inner response.

Some people make important decisions by using the "chance" method. They flip coins, roll dice, or look for signs. The Apostles used this method in selecting someone to take the place of Judas. They selected Justus and Matthias, then prayed and cast lots to see who would be chosen. Although Matthias was selected according to the lots cast, we never hear any more about him. I believe their prayer for guidance in selecting a new Apostle was really answered on the road to Damascus when Saul was converted.

Nothing ever happens by chance, so why leave your decision to chance? Have confidence in your inner Spirit to guide and direct you. Sometimes the sincere Truth student believes he uses this method when he says: "If it doesn't work out, it must not be right for me," or "God doesn't want me to do it." This is not logical. If you are praying for healing and it does not come right away, it is not because God does not want you to be healed. It is always His will for you to be healed. The same applies for prosperity, harmony, peace, and any other good you may be seeking. What you are seeking may be right and in order, but it may also be necessary for you to build the consciousness necessary to manifest the good you are seeking.

One of the first requirements for knowing what is best for you is a complete willingness to let go what you personally think is best for you. The rich young man who asked Jesus how to get into the kingdom of heaven did not really want to know; he wanted to hold on to his wealth. Contrast this with Zacchaeus, the tax collector, who was willing to give up his wealth. Jesus never told him to sell all he had and give it to the poor, as he had told the rich young man. Instead, Jesus spent the night in the home of Zacchaeus. The absence of wealth is no guarantee that one will get divine guidance. Jesus was concerned with attitude. If we have possessive, clinging, prejudiced minds and hearts, we are not open and receptive to divine guidance.

We must want to know and be willing to accept, else we do not receive divine guidance. Can you honestly say to yourself at this moment, *"Not my will, but thine, be done"*? Or can you say as Paul did, *"What shall I do, Lord"*? There is nothing in this world worth clinging to if it keeps you from fully knowing the divine purpose and meaning for your life. Contrary to human traditional opinion, the will of God for you is only good. His will is that which you can follow with eagerness, enthusiasm, joy, and diligence; it will give you the greatest feeling of self-fulfillment and happiness you will ever experience. Some of the things that are required of you may be challenging, but, when you know you are more than equal to all challenges, you will accept them with joy and enthusiasm. You will know that meeting them is a means of greater self-fulfillment.

Willingness to let go of personal plans and to accept new and challenging ideas will help you to fulfill another important requirement for getting divine guidance, and that is to develop the practice of seeking light within yourself rather than in the world of appearances. When you become an inner seeker of light, you will learn to recognize the difference between "intellectual" inspiration and "spiritual" inspiration.

Intellectual inspiration is the excitement we feel when we have mentally formed a frame of reference that seems to offer the possibilities of health, prosperity, or happiness. This "frame of reference" is based on outer appearances. For example, one experiences this intellectual inspiration when he thinks he has found the right partner, or the job that will offer prosperity and security, or a method that offers great wealth or fame and recognition.

Intellectual inspiration has a strong appeal to the senses. It makes you feel that your happiness is dependent upon some person or circumstance. Intellectual inspiration seems promising; it also seems to offer the most benefits for the least effort. It seems that good can be obtained without the necessity of changing one's attitudes, thoughts, feelings, or beliefs. If acted upon, the results are short-lived. Acting upon this intellectual guidance is often detrimental to obtaining further good. When it is not in accord with the spiritual illumination that comes from within, one soon finds himself overwhelmed with problems.

The results that come, both inwardly and outwardly, from following spiritual guidance are long-lasting and dependable. We also find that as we follow our inner leading we are blessed with even greater good in the future.

At first it may seem a big sacrifice to let go of personal desires, but you will find it is not sacrifice at all, for the good that will come into your life will be what you are truly looking for.

As you receive ideas from within, be careful not to analyze them from the human point of view and call them "impractical" or "impossible." Accept them, meditate on them, and you will soon come to realize how practical they are.

One who follows inner guidance in making decisions will be able to meet life confidently. He will have the inner assurance that he is working with God. He does not have to force things to work out in his favor. They will unfold naturally and beautifully. He also finds that he does not have to compete with anyone else; he does not have to drive hard and fast bargains.

There may be times when he will have to stand firm in faith until the outer manifestation comes forth. But the time of waiting will not be a time of frustration, for he will have the inner knowing that the good desired is on the way and nothing can keep it from manifesting.

A prayer that may help you get the divine guidance you seek is this: *God in me is infinite wisdom. He shows me what to do and I do it. I am willing to let go of all preconceived notions of what I think is right and best for me so that God can reveal to me what is truly satisfying.*

The Need for Self-Discipline

The word *discipline* sometimes seems distasteful to us. Some of us don't like to hear it, nor to contemplate what it means. It seems that discipline is often felt to be something harsh, something that will make our lives miserable, unbearable, and joyless; but this is not the case.

A winner is disciplined. Discipline is simply the ability to train ourselves in habits that will contribute to our success and well-being. For example, there are people who are apparent failures, not because they have no talent or ability, but simply because they have never learned to stick to something. They will get started on a project and give up even before they are half finished. In other words, they have good intentions but they lack follow-through.

It takes self-discipline for us to do things we neither want to do nor feel like doing. They may be things we know we should do. They may be things we know will be of benefit to us, and yet we lack the ability to control our habits and our sensory responses to life in order that we might enjoy greater good.

Self-discipline will never take anything away from us; it will enable us to enjoy life more fully. The person who is a victim of undesirable habits is not a happy person, nor can he be a winner, a successful person. He is filled with guilt feelings and frustration.

An undisciplined person wastes a lot of time, effort, and energy in his attempts to achieve success. Starting and stopping uses more energy than continuous movement toward a specific goal. When one is self-disciplined, he knows what must be done and, therefore, all arguments for getting out of the action are avoided and energy is conserved. The undisciplined person flits back and forth; one moment he is going to do something and the next moment he is seeking a way out, an excuse not to do what he knows he should do.

It only takes discipline to get ourselves established in a new habit. Once a habit is established well enough that we perform the action unconsciously, there seems to be no need for discipline—the action is automatic. Much to our surprise, it is not as difficult as it may have seemed in the beginning. Once we break the initial resistance barrier, we are moved along with little effort. The realization of this should encourage us to stick with our projects, for it is when this stage is reached that we get tremendous benefits.

Anytime you undertake a new project or decide to develop a talent there will be a need for discipline. It takes discipline to lose weight. It takes discipline to learn a new subject. It takes discipline to develop muscles through exercise. It takes discipline for any improvement in life. How are we to develop the discipline necessary to win?

It is better to begin with a small project than to tackle something we have been struggling with for a long time. Instead of undertaking something that will take five years of discipline to learn, begin with something that will take only a month or two. For example, if you want to improve your health through exercise, begin by taking simple walks on a regular basis. Don't rush out and buy barbells or gym equipment; don't even join a club. Many people buy health club memberships only to find they lack the discipline to use them on a regular basis. It is better to develop a degree of discipline first. The health club will then be valuable to you.

Another major point: Decide what is truly important to you. After all, you are going to invest time, energy, effort, and possibly even money; you don't want to waste these valuable assets. When I finally got serious about winning at health I knew some type of exercise would have to be incorporated into my daily schedule. I considered barbells, weight-lifting equipment, bicycling, swimming, running, and exercise gadgets for use at home. Tennis and racquetball were also considered, with the idea that the tedium of exercising could be made more pleasant by doing something that seemed to be enjoyable. After considering all the options I could think of, I decided that running was the thing for me. In the beginning, it took considerable self-discipline to get started and to keep at it. There were many times that I almost quit. But I was determined to stick with it through all the aches and pains (there were quite a few of those). But, as my strength developed, the aches and pains disappeared. The more I ran, the easier it became. In the morning, instead of wanting to stay in bed and sleep, I wanted to get up and run. If anyone had ever told me I would one day be getting up at four o'clock for the purpose of running seven to ten miles in below-freezing weather, I would have said he was fantasizing.

Here is an interesting sidelight about discipline: As you become disciplined in one practice there is a carry-over benefit into other areas of your life. You will more easily accomplish other things that you have been putting off. You will be more decisive and procrastinate less. You will discover that it generally takes less time and energy to go ahead and do something than it does to put it off.

Discipline contributes to our peace of mind, self-esteem, and happiness. It adds to our total well-being. In fact, with a little discipline, we find that we can actually enjoy things that seemed unenjoyable, or we can like things that seemed unlikable.

The disciplined person is sometimes accused of being an inflexible person, a square who never enjoys life. It is possible to get carried away and over-discipline, but most of us do not have to be concerned about that! We do need to come to grips with the challenging idea that there will be no winning at anything without some degree of self-discipline.

Many people are running around looking for what I call "overriders"—things they can do, or foods they can eat, or pills they can take to nullify the negative consequences of their undisciplined lives. These overriders will never work to their complete satisfaction. Advertisements appeal to this human desire. For example, one ad stated, "Eat all you want and lose weight." The overrider was a pill that would supposedly nullify the effects of excess calories. In the self-help, motivational, and success-achieving fields we also have to be careful of exaggerated claims of overriders. There will be no success, no winning, no getting something for nothing in the game of life without discipline.

Instead of flitting around from pillar to post, instead of running after every exaggerated claim, instead of seeking to avoid what we know has to be done, exerting a little discipline in the direction we know we should follow will bring fantastic results, far greater than we had imagined.

Life seems to have some very exacting rules, and it is sometimes difficult to live by these. But we should remember that the rules assure success; the more we adhere to them the greater will be the benefits. What good is a fifty-yard pass completion if one of the team members is offsides and the play is called back? Discipline is the ability to play the game of life by the rules—the principles. These principles always lead to success, to beneficial and enjoyable experiences, to a life we can enjoy with peace of mind and freedom from guilt and fear.

Socrates once said, "The unexamined life isn't worth living." I would like to substitute for "unexamined" the word "undisciplined," and rephrase the statement in this way: "The undisciplined life isn't worth living," for there is no real and lasting joy and benefit in scattering our energies, following after every fly-by-night offer of something for nothing.

Life is generous—far more than we know at this moment. As we discipline ourselves to give our best in all we do, life will give back to us abundantly of its blessings.

Give Your Best

If there is anything that will catapult an individual into the winner's circle, it is doing his best in whatever he does. In fact, a person with immense natural talent will be a failure if he does not give his best. He who lets up in this area will surely be let down.

Even in personal growth and development, we must give our best or the results will be disappointing. If we try to increase our strength and physical endurance by exercising half-heartedly once in a while, we will never make it. If we give our best to what we are doing, what we do will be rewarding.

This idea might be classified as "service." There are many opportunities in life to serve, but we don't always take advantage of these opportunities. Most people do not see them as opportunities; if they did, they would not try to escape them or get out of performing the duties required by them. However, when one rises into the winning consciousness of thinking, he sees every opportunity to serve as an opportunity to grow, an opportunity to win in the search for happiness, joy, peace, satisfaction, and many other important values.

Unselfish service was a dominant theme in Jesus' teachings. He stated that the greatest would be the servant, and He included Himself in the category of a servant. He stressed many times that great happiness, peace, joy, and true fulfillment in life can come only in giving of ourselves unselfishly.

Several years ago, when I was looking for a church secretary, a young woman applied. The first things she asked about were the benefits of the job—the salary, vacation time, sick leave, and even termination pay. She was more interested in what she would receive than in what the job was and what she would be doing. I felt like asking her, "And what do you propose to do? What type of fringe benefits are you prepared to give to the job?" She apparently had the attitude that life and the system owed her a comfortable living without her putting forth much effort. She probably had no intention of giving her best to that job or any job. Even if she had been talented and could handle the job, she would not have succeeded with this attitude.

Many people are afflicted with this negative concept of life—that life owes them a living or that the system, the government, owes them a guaranteed life of health and prosperity. Life is generous, but it does not owe anyone anything; it will not give its blessings without some effort on our part. It may seem that life's demands are rigorous and difficult, but they really are not. When we get involved with giving instead of withholding, we find that tremendous things can be accomplished with very little effort.

Albert Einstein has said, *The high destiny of the individual is to serve rather than to rule, or impose himself in any other way.* He was an individual who certainly sought to give his best, and, because of this, mankind has been richly blessed. He was a winner, and he is telling us that serving is the royal road to winning in life.

Jesus also stressed this idea when He said, *". . . give, and it will be given to you; good measure, pressed down, shaken together, running over. . . . "* He did not say that we should wait until we get something, for He knew we already had something to give, and He was not referring to money. We can actually begin by asking, "To what am I giving my time, my thought, and my energy right now?" When I seriously asked myself that question, I got some disturbing answers. I discovered I was giving all my valuable time to things that were not only non-productive but in some instances downright depleting, such as watching television hour after hour and eating snacks constantly. What possible good could life give back to me for the time and effort expended in that way?

Do you enjoy your work? Do you enjoy it so much that you would be willing to do it even without pay? Or do you see your work as just a means of getting wealth or of maintaining an existence? Do you give your best to what you are doing? Do you sometimes withhold doing something because you are not paid for doing it, or because it is someone else's duty? Are you seeking to get the advantages and benefits for the least amount of effort? Do you ever stop to ask how you can give more to your work, how you can improve it, how you can increase your capacity to do more and thereby increase your productivity?

You may now ask another question of me: "Why should I give all this time, energy, and creative effort to a company that is taking advantage of me? They get all the profits and I get nothing." First of all, you are not just working for a company. You are self-employed, you are working for your life. Second, life will give back to you, it will prosper you in some way, through the company to which you give the service or in some other way. This is often referred to as the principle of *compensation.* If you will give your best where you are, you will be rewarded in some way.

The person who continually gives his best cannot stand still and he cannot be held back; life will propel him onward and upward. He will surely find greater success. Whereas before it seemed as though life was holding him back, now it will be thrusting him forward.

Trying to get something for nothing is like trying to swim against the current. Lying, stealing, cheating, taking unfair advantage of others, even when permitted by the laws, is swimming against the current of life. Eventually it will have disastrous effects.

One swimming with the current enjoys the bliss of winning, the joy of serving, the assurance of knowing that he will always be taken care of, that life will always provide for him. If he has to start out applying this principle in an area of work that he does not particularly enjoy, he will soon find himself transferred to one he does enjoy.

The way to greater blessings is through greater service. We must make an agreement with ourselves to make service our primary goal. Many people work but do not serve. We can begin right where we are and make our work a "service project." By serving, we give our best efforts with love and concern for what we do. J. C. Penney once said, *Employees who give no more of their time and interest than sheer necessity demands do not comprehend a vital principle which is as true in business as in the spiritual realm; namely, that a man must "lose his life in order to save it." In other words, he must forget himself in service.* Serve, give your best, and you will be compensated far above the monetary blessings you might receive. Service will open the door to advancement—the opportunity to serve in a greater capacity.

It is amazing how much time some people spend and how much potential creative thought energy they waste trying to figure out ways to do less, to avoid working or serving. This is the way to stay behind. A winner is always interested in getting ahead, improving, advancing, helping, serving. He therefore uses his valuable creative thought energy seeking ways to do more, to give more, to be more; and as a result he accomplishes more. When opportunities open up for him, some may say it is fate or fortune. Seldom do these people see that it was just the result of constructively giving himself to life. If they would do the same thing, opportunities would open up for them.

Every opportunity to serve, no matter how menial the task may seem to be, is an opportunity for advancement in life. Many times those menial tasks will lead to something far greater than we had expected.

If you will do what is before you to the best of your ability and with the greatest concern and interest, as if it were your very own, you will be astonished at the many blessings that will come your way. These will be not only material blessings, but, even more important, the inner blessings of joy, peace, security, and happiness in what you are doing.

43

Relaxing in a World
of Pressure

People spend a lot of time and money trying to relax—some fish, some play golf, some scuba dive, some ski, some sit in a tub of hot water, some get massages, some flop in front of the television, and some take tranquilizers. Some have more constructive methods, such as hobbies, that absorb their interest to the extent that they do not think negatively about their problems.

We live in a pressure-filled world. We compete for jobs and for the goods of the world. The intense negative thinking and emotions that many entertain regarding these competitive items makes them tense, and they cannot relax mentally, emotionally, or physically.

Some persons say that life is getting so complex and so fast that they cannot keep up. This type of thinking also makes us tense and frustrated. But we cannot turn back or escape from life, and neither should we resist it. There are many things we cannot change.

How are we to cope with the many pressures? How can we live relaxed and peaceful lives in a world of pressures? How can we deal effectively with the build-up of inner stress? Is it possible to reduce stress and be relaxed? The answer is yes. Here are four ideas that may help defuse negative thinking when you are confronted with a potential pressure situation.

The first point is: When we find ourselves getting worked up over any situation, we should immediately stop all negative thinking and analysis and begin to affirm: *Divine order is now established in this situation.* This is acknowledging and claiming divine intervention, which is the desire to accept and express wisdom and love. With God there is always a right and harmonious solution to every problem or challenge. Affirming divine order, which will work in any situation or need, gives a new direction to our thinking. It will help us let go all negative analysis of the situation.

For example, if one needs employment, instead of fretting and worrying, he should affirm divine order. Divine order means there is a right place of service already prepared for the individual, and this is true regardless of age or what the unemployment figures indicate. Divine order is acknowledging that God will guide us to our rightful places. Divine order for health is affirming that God's life and intelligence bring about a rightful working relationship in the physical body. It is the acknowledgment that healing is possible. Divine order is the right solution, the divine solution, for any problem.

Second, when we find ourselves confronted with a negative personality situation, we can think of it impersonally. Many people give a personal interpretation to everything that happens in their lives. For example, they may say something like, "God doesn't love me," or "My parents and friends don't care," or "They don't pay me enough because they don't appreciate me," or, when someone passes them on the street and looks at them in the wrong way, they will say, "What did you mean by that?"

These personal interpretations build up anxiety and frustration and cause stress and tension. We should always remind ourselves that our happiness is not dependent on another's opinion of us. We should not limit our happiness and our good in life simply because someone has a negative personal interpretation of us and what we might be doing. We certainly should not feel that we cannot be happy simply because someone has rejected us. We cannot determine our worth in life by the position we happen to be in, just as we cannot determine our potential by some so-called IQ test. We are where we are because we have not realized our great potential. As soon as we do, the outer will change to correspond with our new perspective.

All personal assessments are limited. The impersonal is based on principle and not on so-called facts. What God thinks of me is principle and is impersonal. What someone else thinks of me is only a factual opinion that may be distorted; it is very personal. The same thing applies to what I might think of myself on the personal level. Because of certain experiences, especially unhappy ones, a person may feel inadequate and believe he lacks talent and ability to succeed in life. So he should be careful not to accept these personal, limiting assessments.

Why should we accept someone's assessment of us since most personal assessments are limited in the first place? What we think of ourselves is far more important than what others think of us. We can control what we think about ourselves, whereas we cannot control others' views. But we can refuse to accept others' views and opinions about us.

The third point is: Instead of using force to bring about a right solution to a problem that is causing stress, we can seek to use persuasion. It is especially true in personality situations that the best way to defuse personality pressures is to persuade with loving understanding. We may be in a position where we can use personal force to make someone submit to our will, but we will not win the cooperation and support of the other person or persons. We will never lose through persuasion, but we will always lose through the force of will. The first loss is the inability to be at ease about the personal relationship. We will have to be on guard against possible retribution. We must recognize that people have to grow into a higher realization; we cannot force them into one. We must appeal to their higher self instead of focusing on their shortcomings.

Fourth, we can always be assured that prayer will help us. When we are disturbed we should pray or meditate—close our eyes to the person or the problem and be still. Nothing can be solved by our thinking about it and analyzing it and trying to figure out why it happened or why someone did what he did. Be still and let God think through you. Your mind may want to search for answers, but tell it to be still. God has the answer, and He will reveal it to you. Never try to force things to work out to satisfy your personal desire. Relax and let God bring forth the right and harmonious answer through you.

When our thoughts and feelings are relaxed through thinking about peaceful ideas, the body will relax. We will feel peaceful and calm. All the processes that the body must perform will be done more easily. This feeling will be expressed in statements such as, "I feel great," and "Life is wonderful." It feels great to feel good, to experience release from the pressures of our world.

Winning at Health

The body is a marvelous organism. If we really understood it, we would be amazed at how great its renewing powers are. It is constantly seeking to rejuvenate itself. The natural condition for the body is to be healthy, vital, energetic, and youthful. If we so desire, we can work with this natural tendency and bring about fantastic improvements in our physical and mental well-being.

If we are seriously to seek better health, we must come to grips with some startling and challenging ideas about health. The first one is this: The causes of ill health are not so much outside ourselves as they are in our attitudes and beliefs. What we think and feel have a definite influence upon the physical body. For example, when a person becomes angry, a detrimental chemical action begins to take place in the body. Acids are secreted into the system. If this persists over a period of time, this acid can erode some part of the body, for example, the stomach, and a person may develop an ulcer.

Every action of thought, positive or negative, initiates a chemical action in the body. Anger, tension, stress, and anxiety can affect the heartbeat and blood circulation. These conditions can in turn affect other parts of the body. This mental/emotional influence

51

upon the body is called *psychosomatic*; it is now believed that as much as eighty percent of all physical conditions are psychosomatic. That is just a fancy way of saying that our thinking, feeling, and believing affect our bodies in some way, either positively or negatively.

Therefore, it is imperative that we make a concerted effort to control our thinking. We must recondition ourselves so that our automatic responses to negative situations are positive instead of negative. Negative responses are not natural but learned responses, and because of this we can unlearn, retrain, or recondition ourselves with positive and constructive responses. It will take effort, but it is effort that will pay rich dividends in the form of better health. Of course some will prefer to suffer the physical pain and take some medicine to relieve the physical condition. That is a tremendous price to pay for the privilege of negative indulgence.

When a person thinks negatively, there is another phenomenon that intensifies and encourages a physical limitation. The negative chemical stimulation creates cravings for certain types of foods that are detrimental but when ingested seem to have a pleasurable and soothing effect. For example, negative thinking and the negative expression of our feelings are enervating, for they consume more than the normal amount of energy. For a quick pickup of energy, an individual may eat some candy and feel better for a time. However, this quick pickup does not last long, so the individual eats another one, and it does not take long to develop a habit of dependence. Such a habit overworks the physical body. Not only must the body seek to eliminate the overabundance of unneeded and undesired chemicals from the negative stimulation, but it must now work to eliminate, control, and seek to balance the input from the candy.

When we stop to consider the substance we put into our system for pickups and stimulation, we must realize that the body is working overtime trying to deal with this unnecessary material. It takes energy to deal with this waste, and it takes time. Before all of it can be dealt with, a person may further abuse himself. When this happens, accumulations begin to take place, not only in the form of extra weight but also accumulations of waste material that the body cannot eliminate. This waste material builds up in joints and other areas, producing aches and pains.

Trying to overcome the pain, some individuals take drugs to feel better. This only adds to the accumulation of chemicals that the body must eliminate. There may be temporary relief from the pain, but no healing takes place.

A person can get so used to pickups and stimulants that he feels he cannot be comfortable or enjoy life without them; any suggestion that they be eliminated is often rejected. The solution is not just to eliminate the outer stimulants. The solution lies in developing a positive and constructive way of thinking and responding to the challenges of life so that we do not create the need for stimulants in the first place. When the two work together, radical improvement can be brought about quickly in one's health.

When a person finds himself in a frustrating situation, there are three ways he can deal with it. He can change the situation, get out of it, or move to another location; he can repress his negative emotional responses and learn to adapt or live with it; or he can develop a positive and constructive attitude of understanding and non-resistance. Instead of internalizing the negative opinions or assuming the worst about the situation, the individual, through prayer, develops a positive way of thinking. This is the way of the winner. He knows that what he thinks, the way he responds emotionally, will have some type of effect upon his energy level and his health.

For example, when someone does something offensive, the winner seeks to understand and forgive instead of retaliating with anger and resentment. Forgiveness is more than toleration or putting up with something. That is the way of the second method. Forgiveness is a genuine expression of love. To be able to forgive, one must realize that, while nothing is lost in forgiving, much is gained; but much is lost in resentment. Not only does one lose peace of mind, he will eventually lose his health. By forgiving, one maintains peace, poise, control, and good health.

You no doubt have heard the statement, or you may have made it yourself, referring to a negative person, "He makes me sick." It is not the person himself that makes one sick but negative thinking about the person. Since we have the power and ability to control our thinking, we can train ourselves to think on higher levels. When we learn to control our thoughts and feelings, we call this maturity.

When a person is in a good, positive, and constructive state of consciousness and watches what he puts into his body, he finds that he is in such a state of health that his body can withstand any onslaught of germs that may be present in his environment. Others may have colds and the flu, but he does not. It is not the germs that cause the colds, it is the weakened condition of the body that provides them the opportunity to do their damaging work.

During the past few years I have read many books on nutrition and health. I felt I was losing the struggle for good health, and I was seriously seeking a way to rejuvenation. Some of what has already been said comes out of my personal experiences. I have experimented on myself, and I have discovered some things that may be controversial, but they work for me. I offer them here as a help, and in no way do I mean to depreciate the value of some things that people believe to be helpful.

I realized that I must cease putting into my body things that it does not need, things that only make it work overtime to eliminate. What things? To name a few: coffee, sugar, honey, alcohol, chocolate, white bread, pastries of all types, and ice cream. You may think you cannot enjoy life without some of these things, but I assure you that I have found life more enjoyable without them. I do not miss them, and I do not feel I am missing out on anything when I have a meal without dessert.

Another thing I have discovered is that we eat far too much food. My energy level has increased dramatically by eliminating the negative foods I have mentioned and by decreasing my food intake. How can one increase his energy level while at the same time decreasing the amount of food and increasing the physical demands upon the body by vigorous exercise, such as running? I think the answer is simply *efficiency.* When the negative demands upon the body are eliminated, it works more efficiently, and the individual has energy to spare.

I remember when I played football in high school, the coach gave us salt tablets. It was believed that the salt lost through perspiration had to be replaced. Now, even though I can run steadily without stopping for as long as two and a half hours, perspiring profusely, I do not take any salt tablets nor do I use salt on foods. I find that extra salt is not needed.

My overall health is excellent—no aches or pains, and I have peaceful, restful sleep at night. My energy level has increased. Recovery time after physical exertion is rapid, which means I need less sleep and therefore have more time to pursue my interests and studies. One thing that is especially enjoyable is the increased keenness of mind. It feels great to feel good! I have also won the battle of the bulge, and I do not have to concern myself with the frustration of trying to follow a diet I do not like. I enjoy good, healthful foods.

There is a great interest in body rejuvenation today, and this is wonderful. It means that we are coming to realize the importance of the body. I certainly do not have all the answers. However, I have found some things that work for me, and I like the results. I am open and receptive to further growth, and I will keep on seeking greater insight into this wonderful temple in which we live. If you will seek within yourself, your own indwelling Spirit will tell you what you should do to have and enjoy better health. Listen and follow that guidance no matter what the authorities in the outer world say. *You can win at health.*

The Practice of Meditation

One secret to successful living is in the daily practice of meditation. Through regular periods of meditation we find new inspiration to meet the challenges of life, and we receive the guidance we need to help us achieve our goals. Through meditation we gain the faith, courage, health, and assurance of supply that make us winners.

True meditation is communion with God, the creative Intelligence within us. Meditation is more than an intellectual exercise, even though that exercise is beneficial and helpful in achieving true meditation. It is not a time of begging, beseeching, or asking for personal favors. It is especially not a time to ask God to change the laws of the universe for us. True meditation is a time of quietly receiving inspiration and illumination from God. It is rising out of human thought with all of its outlining of personal requests and entering into an idealized consciousness of intuitive thought. Einstein has said that intuitive thinking is the highest type of thought in which we can be involved.

In this consciousness of the presence of God, one does not think of things as they are. He does not dwell on the negative aspects of his life nor the lives of those dear to him. He does not analyze his problems and attempt to tell God how to solve them. In this higher consciousness, he lets God think through him in the form of ideas and inspiration.

Books and teachers can help us learn about meditation, but we will have to do the actual work. Teachers cannot meditate for us; we must do it for ourselves. Therefore, we must learn our own individual technique. There is really only one Teacher, and He is within you. He will teach you all you need to know and give you answers that no one outside of you can give.

Genuine prayer is an experience in which we surpass our limited human thought about ourselves. In true meditation we see ourselves not as human beings but as spiritual beings. Instead of thinking of ourselves as losers, we think of ourselves as winners. How can we lose when we have the backing and support of God? In meditation we begin to realize our true potential, not all of it at once, but more and more each day, and we begin to use this potential to achieve the goals we are inspired to achieve.

How can we enter into this consciousness of true meditation? The first thing to do is to get into a comfortable position where the body is not a distracting influence, preferably a place where it is quiet and you can be alone without any disturbances from family, television, phone calls, or visitors.

The work begins in the conscious mind. This may be a rather challenging thing to do, but it is necessary: *Develop the willingness to completely release all your present personal desires and beliefs.* This includes those cherished beliefs that you already think are true. You must be willing even to let go of your thinking about the need for healing, prosperity, or some other good you are seeking. You are not seeking this power to use it but to let it use you. When you achieve this, all the other things will be added with much less effort; they will be by-products of your working with the creative Intelligence within you. If you seek God just for the benefit of healing, you will not find Him, even though in this seeking you may find a degree of physical improvement. You see, it is possible to achieve a degree of healing through the use of mental suggestion in the same way that we can bring about sickness through mental suggestion.

At first it may seem that in giving up your personal desires you are going to lose your last hope of happiness in this world. But do not fear that. We all have personal desires that we think will make us happy and successful and even healthy. You will discover that, when you are willing to let go of those personal desires, the desires that are for your highest good will be fulfilled. As for the others, you will rejoice in being free from them.

Until we come to grips with personal desire and become completely willing to let go, it is useless to practice the succeeding steps in meditation. When the desire to know God supersedes all desire to gain in the outer, we are ready to take the next step.

That next step will be the setting of a time in your daily schedule for being completely alone. You must never rationalize, saying, "I don't have time for meditation." If it seems you do not have time, you must make time. Nothing is more important than your effort to know God. In your first attempts to be quiet, you may be bored and restless, and the desire for

59

sensory stimulation may seem almost overwhelming. It will be helpful to begin your meditation by reading an inspirational book or by repeating affirmations. If you are faithful in your efforts each day, you will find that the desire for sensory stimulation will decrease.

The time of day that you wish to be alone is up to you. However, it should be a time that is free of outer demands and preferably the same time each day. It may be that you will want to set your clock and get up earlier for this special time.

After you have some of these preliminary details worked out and you are alone, then you will begin a mental and emotional discipline necessary to meditation. When you seek to become still, you may find your mind wandering. You may have a tendency to think about all the details of your life—your work, your health, your relatives, and many other things. Some of these things may seem to be serious problems that you feel need your attention, but they do not need your attention in meditation. You will not have to tell God all the negative details; you never have to tell Him anything, for He knows all. So you can confidently let this concerned thinking go, or at least make the effort to let it go. Do not resist these thoughts, but gently and firmly take control of your thinking by repeating some affirmative thoughts such as the following:

I am now free of all personal desire. I am at peace. Nothing can disturb me mentally or emotionally, for I know that You are in charge of my life and my affairs. I trust You absolutely in all things. I now let go all concern about my family and friends. I know that You are within them to guide them and take care of them.

Knowing this and trusting You to care for them is the greatest blessing I can give them. I forgive all offenses and release all emotional resentment. I have no desire to get even with anyone for any reason. I am completely open and receptive to anything that You wish to reveal to me. I am listening.

This preliminary to meditation is called *contemplation.* It is only a suggestion. You can develop your own ideas according to the need of your consciousness. Whatever statements you affirm, they should include the ideas of release, peace, forgiveness, and open-minded receptivity.

In the beginning you may find that most of the time you have set aside for meditation is taken up with the physical, mental, and emotional disciplines and little time is left for complete "listening," or, as it is often called, the Silence. Do not be disturbed by this. As you persistently practice meditation you will gain control of your thoughts and feelings and the time for complete "listening" will increase.

I would caution you about attempting to make your mind a complete blank. Doing this tends to focus the mind on the very thing that you want to release and creates a feeling of resistance, which is detrimental to achieving true meditation. Attempting to "blank out" the mind creates a mental vacuum and opens the door for negative thoughts to come in. Positive control of the process of thinking is developed through self-discipline. You choose what you desire to think about. When the conscious mind is lifted to a level of nobler thinking, negative thoughts will not interfere.

After you have achieved a degree of success, you may find that during your "listening" period you tend to go to sleep. If this happens, take it in your stride and give thanks for it. It means you are learning to relax and let go. It will probably be the most refreshing sleep you have ever had. Just keep up the daily practice. Eventually you will achieve the true "listening" state of mind. There will be no racing thoughts or emotions. There will be inner calmness and stillness that you had never thought possible. Even though you are in a conscious state, you will not be disturbed by the sounds around you. Your mind will be focused inwardly in rapt attention.

In these early stages of the practice of meditation, you may have only a deep sense of peace. There may be no new ideas revealed on the conscious level, and you may be wondering if you are ever going to get the guidance or the help you need in dealing with the outside affairs of your life. Be patient. You will find that you will receive ideas as you go about your daily tasks, ideas that might not have come to you if you had not had the earlier quiet time. Another thing, in these times of meditation, a great deal of illuminating work is going on in the unconscious realm of mind. Beliefs and attitudes must be changed in the unconscious before outer changes take place. So be patient, faithful, and trusting.

If you are persistent in your daily practice of meditation, you will find that you are changing, both in your attitudes toward yourself, others, and your world, and outward things will begin to improve. You will discover that your interests and tastes for things, places, actions, and people will undergo radical change. It will not be through an act of willpower but it will be a harmonious change. In some instances the outer will remain the same, but those outer people and conditions will no longer disturb you.

With this type of control of your thoughts and emotions, you will be receptive to the dynamic ideas that will help you be the winner you desire to be.

The Search for Happiness

One of the things the United States Constitution guarantees is "the pursuit of happiness." Most people pursue it, though they may not know what it is they seek. The government does not tell us what happiness is and cannot tell us how to find it. It only says that we are free to search for it to our heart's content. The government cannot give it to us, for it is an unknown variable. What one person calls happiness may be totally objectionable to another person. The government cannot even provide the right environment for us to experience happiness. Even if the government could provide adequate housing, income, education, and all the other desirables of our culture, this would in no way guarantee that we would find happiness.

No one can give us happiness or make us happy. Some people search for an ideal companion, thinking that in the perfect relationship they will find happiness. Some people are searching for an ideal place to live where they can be happy. If you were to put such people in the environment of their choice, I predict that they still would not be completely happy. Some look for ideal work with the highest pay, thinking they will be happy if all their needs are met easily with some left over for entertainment. But even this will not make anyone happy. Only the individual can make himself happy.

Happiness is not found just in achieving some challenging goal. When the goal is reached, the happiness ends. This should begin to tell us something about the nature of happiness, but I believe we have overlooked the simple truth. We cannot live in the past, relishing past accomplishments, thinking we will be happy vicariously. Amassing wealth will not make anyone happy, but this does not mean that getting rid of wealth and taking vows of poverty will make a person happy either. It is good and pleasant to have wealth, and one should have enough to do the things he likes to do and to express the ideas he knows he should express. But wealth of itself will not make us happy.

To be happy is to *be* something rather than to *have* something. Happiness is that genuinely good feeling we experience when we know and express what is right, true, good, and beautiful. Even if the whole world loved us, we might not be happy. But when we *express* the principle of love, we are happy, and we will maintain our happiness even if we are rejected by the world. Happiness is something, therefore, that you can experience without a reason for it.

Being what you were created to be will cause you to experience constant happiness, a happiness that does not fluctuate with world conditions.

There are at least four important things we should remember in our search for happiness. *First, we must find oneness with God.* When we know God within us as our help in every need, then and only then will we begin to know what happiness is all about. Our lives may be in tatters at the moment, but we will be

66

happy; for happiness, as I have said, is not dependent upon some outer condition, but it is dependent upon this first inner condition—a realization of oneness with God. It does not have to be any more than a simple awareness of the truth that God is within us and that we are never separated from Him.

There is no human or physical experience to compare with the feeling of joy and happiness we experience when we realize that God is within us to guide us, to sustain us, and to help us in our time of need. We may have been filled with joy and excitement on the occasion of some special event, such as a marriage or the birth of a child, but it will never compare with the feeling of happiness of just knowing and being able to affirm in faith: *I am one with God.*

With this inner awareness of God's presence, there is no feeling of loneliness, even though we may be alone. Many search among the crowds for someone to love them or to keep them company, but even in a crowd they are lonely. To live in the consciousness that God is with us to guide and help us is lasting happiness. We are happy with successes and accomplishments, and we are happy in the preparation and work that go into achieving them. Things may come and things may go, but happiness is enduring.

There may and will be many challenges, but they cannot destroy our happiness. There may and will be people expressing human qualities and doing human things, but they will not have the power to destroy the happy feeling that comes through the awareness of God in consciousness.

Second, happiness is a mind free to know the truth

and to express it. The writer of Proverbs says: *Happy is the man who finds wisdom, and the man who gets understanding.* A mind that is free from the necessity to argue and prove theological, political, social, and cultural beliefs and attitudes is a mind that is open and capable of receiving, considering, and accepting new ideas about life and about the world in which we live. It is amazing how often people get upset at the mere mention of any idea that is opposed to their way of thinking and believing. If they were secure in their beliefs, there would be no need to argue. Happiness is knowing the truth and expressing it. Happiness is the process of searching for the truth that we do not as yet know. Happiness is the expectation of finding more and more of the great truths about life.

Third, happiness is giving instead of just receiving. This is a challenging thought, for we have been conditioned to believe that happiness comes from acquiring many things. In our society we are led to believe that we cannot be happy until we receive the best that society has to offer in worldly goods. So many people sit around in misery waiting to receive, moaning over what they do not have. Some are bold and demand more, thinking they will be happy when they get more. Still others are even bolder and more foolish and impatient—they go out and take what they want.

If you want to be happy, just give some useful service with no thought of return, and something wonderful will happen in you. To do the work that we are paid for with a generous attitude will help us to experience happiness. To think of how we can do more instead of just receive more is happiness. Many people are unhappy because they are constantly thinking that they are being used or that someone or something is taking advantage of them. If they understood the law of compensation, they would be happy in the knowledge that good always returns to the one who gives it.

Fourth, happiness is growing instead of stagnating. Life is a continuous educational experience. You may have finished school, but you have not finished learning. We should never be satisfied with any level of achievement, especially when we know there is so much to learn and such a great need to continually grow and unfold. Each accomplishment is a preparation for a still greater accomplishment. We should give more thought and time to self-improvement, to the overcoming of undesirable habits, to the learning of self-discipline and self-control. There is no happiness in life without these. Many spend a great deal of effort, thought, and emotion telling others how they should change and improve, yet they are unwilling to change and grow themselves. The happy person is the one who is concerned with his own self-improvement and growth. A winner does not think about what someone else needs to do, he thinks about what he needs to do in order to improve. Stagnation or deterioration is misery, but continual growth and self-improvement are happiness.

So why not get busy and learn something? Learn more about the things you are interested in. Get more than just a superficial knowledge. It may take effort to wade through the reams of books and magazines and to listen to lecturers in order to get a deeper understanding, but you will soon find this to be an enjoyable learning experience. The happy feeling will stay with you and urge you on to even greater pursuits of knowledge.

Every little accomplishment makes you a winner, so always be appreciative of even small improvements. These are the foundations upon which great victories will be won in the future. Cherish and give thanks for them, and continue to work and develop them.

A winner is a participator in life rather than a spectator. He gets into life and lives and grows with it. Put your heart into something, and you will experience the great feeling we are all seeking—happiness.

Your Words Are Powerful

The words we speak each day, orally and mentally, are much more powerful than we have realized. If we did realize their great creative or destructive power, we would be much more diligent in watching what we think and speak.

Words can build or destroy. Just observe another person's reaction to words. When he is praised, he is jubilant. When he is condemned, he is downcast. Isaiah told us of the power of words when he said: *. . . So shall my word be that goes forth from my mouth; it shall not return to me empty, but it shall accomplish that which I purpose, and prosper in the thing for which I sent it.*

All our words are sent somewhere to accomplish some purpose. They are either sent consciously with full deliberation or unconsciously without any disciplined effort to be certain that they are worthy ones. Many words pass through our consciousness each day—words about ourselves, others, our work, our social life, the world in general, and about many miscellaneous subjects. We speak many words in responding to people and life's challenges and opportunities. We read thousands upon thousands of words each day, and we listen to many as well.

Many of the words that pass through our thinking

are negative. For example, when a person reads a typical novel, many negative thoughts and suggestions pass through his mind. When people gossip, negativity passes in and out of their consciousness.

We are constantly responding to the words we experience, the ones we generate and the ones that come from others, and our response will be either negative or positive.

As these words pass through our consciousness, they do so with varying degrees of intensity. As we contemplate them, we can either increase this intensity or dissolve it. It may be that some of these words do not arouse us at all. This can be true of positive and constructive words, as well as negative ones.

However, the words we dwell upon with great intensity are the ones that motivate us either to action or inaction. A winner is motivated to positive and constructive action because he dwells upon words of success, achievement, and accomplishment. He talks about his goals in a positive and constructive manner. In fact, he talks and thinks about everything in his life, as far as he is consciously able, in a positive manner; and this is why he wins at the game of life.

If we examine the words of a loser, we discover that they are negative, doubtful, pessimistic, discouraging, and fatalistic. In his thinking and speaking, nothing is right, nothing will work, and he knows he cannot do much or achieve much. He is an unhappy person, and it was not circumstances that made him that way, it was the words he chose to think and speak. He may think he had no choice, but he did. A winner may be in similar negative circumstances, but he does not let those circumstances determine how he will think and speak and project his words, for he knows, if not consciously, then at least unconsciously, the power of the spoken word, the motivating power of the word.

Words are vocal manifestations of our thoughts and feelings, our attitudes and beliefs. They reveal our personality and our consciousness. As we talk, our words reveal what we are concentrating our productive energy on, and by this we can determine the results we can expect. Here are five suggestions on how to use the power of your word for constructive purposes:

Always respond to negative words in a constructive way. When someone says something insulting, instead of personalizing and taking the words as true, realize it is only an interpretation, revealing his negative frustrations and attitudes, not yours. The key is to depersonalize all negative words directed at you. Criticism can hurt you only if you take it personally. You can control your reaction. What do you do if there is some substance or legitimacy in the criticism? You can either rationalize and resent it and strike back defensively, which is never advisable, or you can accept it constructively and do something to correct it. Holding a resenting word in consciousness is like holding a hot coal in your hand. Let resentment go as quickly as you would drop the hot coal.

Make a conscious effort to watch your words, but not to the extent of being a fanatic. Remember, the suggestion is that you watch *your* words and not those of others. We have enough to deal with in trying to watch what *we* think and say. Clean up your conversation. Attempt to get the negative expressions out of your consciousness. They often come to the surface when we are meeting some challenge. Talk about good ideas, read positive, constructive books and magazines, and listen to positive words on cassettes and if possible on radio and television. Especially watch your words when you are a little "heated up." If you will do this, you will not have to say to yourself later, "I wish I hadn't said that." Work toward the expression, "I am glad I said that." Talk about your good health instead of an illness, no matter how you feel. If someone tries to induce you to talk about your aches and pains, change the subject. Remember, you intensify the things you talk about, for you are speaking the word.

Talk about good times even if you are at the moment experiencing a financial challenge or a success challenge. Talk and think success instead of failure, and you will build the consciousness to make success a fact in your life. It is especially important to learn to think and speak positive and constructive words when we confront appearances and situations that seem threatening. Talking negatively about events before us will not change them, but positive, dynamic, constructive thoughts and words will.

Speak good, positive, constructive words silently. You may want to call this silent autosuggestion. We cannot always express our thoughts vocally to others, for they may not be receptive. If, at a time such as this, you will keep your thoughts positive and dynamically constructive, you will be surprised at the response within the person to whom you are speaking. Send out negative criticism and you will get a negative response. Send out thought and word projections of peace, harmony, love, and respect and you will get a constructive and positive response.

In trying to help other people, do not be too specific or assert that they do exactly what you think they should. We have no right to exert this type of mental influence over others. Leave them free to follow their own inclinations, and in this way you will maintain your freedom from mental domination of others.

The words we speak are not limited by time or space. The word is instantly omnipresent even to the farthest reaches of the universe. The one you pray for does not have to be in your presence to be helped. The same applies for any need. Prayer is the positive power of the spoken word, provided one prays in faith, believing.

Speak your words aloud when you can. Get by yourself and do this, but do not tell others what you are doing. Speak them with strong, powerful vocal conviction. The more sensory avenues you use to impress these words on your subconscious mind, the better and quicker will be the results. Some people have found that putting autosuggestive words to music helps impress them on the subconscious mind. Long after they have ceased speaking, the words continue their silent work in their thoughts. This is the technique the advertising industry uses to persuade people to buy certain products. If it did not work, those big companies would not spend the tremendous sums of money they spend on this type of advertising. With television, they have both sight and sound working for them. You can use this technique by developing your own "advertising copy" of what you want to be, to do, and to have.

75

Remember, the words you project affect you first. Send out what you want to come back. Speak the words that reflect ideas you want to experience or situations you would like to see manifest in your life. Your words are messengers. They will draw people you need to help you, even if you do not know who they are to be. They will draw the substance and the opportunities you need to fulfill yourself in life. Remember the words of Isaiah: *They will not return to me empty.* Your words will return laden with blessings or burdens. The choice is up to you.

You have the power to select your experiences, for you have the power to select your words and the power to select your thoughts. Choose words that ennoble and build up, words that bring forth peace and harmony. People will respond to words of praise and approval much faster than they will to words of so-called constructive criticism. Speak words of love. Send them out on the wavelengths of the universe, and others will feel them. The world is starving more for constructive words of Truth than for food. There is great power in your words, power for greater good for you and for others.

The Magnetism of the Mind

In some respects our minds are similar to magnets—they draw to us experiences that are related to our habitual thoughts. However, there is one major discrepancy in this analogy: With a magnet, unlikes attract, but with the mind, like attracts like. A consciousness that is made up of positive beliefs and attitudes will attract positive and beneficial experiences. A consciousness of negative beliefs and attitudes will attract negative, unpleasant, and undesirable experiences.

Since we are not totally charged one way or the other, we have some of both types of experiences. We may not consciously understand what particular beliefs or attitudes or past experiences are related to some present experience, but we can be sure there is a relationship. Nothing happens by chance.

When we understand this power and use it constructively, we can attract many wonderful experiences into our lives. A winner has a positively charged mind. He thinks success, has goals, and believes he can achieve those goals. He is willing to put forth the effort necessary to accomplish the desires of his heart. His mind becomes so charged, like a magnet, that his good is drawn to him and he to his good.

The average person uses only a very small portion of his potential mind power. What is worse, many people use the power of their minds to identify themselves with negative experiences. The same energy of thought used to manifest some negative experience could be used to manifest something dynamic and positive.

You may ask, "How can I condition my mind constructively in order that I may draw to myself good experiences?" One of the first ways is through doing what you are doing right now, reading a book that offers constructive ideas about life, about you and what you can do. When we consider the negative things we present to the mind each day through radio, television, newspapers, books, and magazines, it is no wonder that many people question whether there is any good in life.

Another method is through the power of affirmation, which is also called autosuggestion. Keep affirming the thing that you wish to experience. The individual who keeps saying "I can" when confronted with a challenge, will find a way to meet that challenge; he will win. The individual who keeps saying "I can't" or "it's too hard" will lose out. He will lose not because it was too hard, but because he thought it was.

What we think on the conscious level, especially with strong feeling, influences the subconscious mind. Positive thought and feeling activity charges the consciousness and will draw good to us. Anyone can achieve the better things in life through positive thought. We do not have to have money to do it. We do not even have to have good health to do it. Though we will probably be surprised to find that it improves our health!

One exciting thought about the magnetic power of the mind is: It is not limited by time or space. If other people are to be involved in the successful completion of our plans, they will be drawn to us even if they are long distances away. People do not just drop into our lives and get involved in our experiences; they come to complete some pattern of thought and desire in our consciousness. This is why it is very important to desire only that which is beneficial for you and for anyone else. We should never desire anything detrimental for anyone; instead, always wish for them the best.

This higher type of thought will give an even more powerful charge to our consciousness, and the good that is drawn into our lives will be a blessing.

Winning at Prosperity

With the continual and rapid rise in inflation it is important to learn winning ways regarding supply and prosperity. If we are to lay a proper foundation for winning at prosperity, we must begin with the premise that it is *possible* for us to be prosperous and to be so regardless of economic fluctuations. It is essential to believe that it is possible, in spite of seeming opposition, for us to be prosperous.

Many people assume that because of their "unique" situation it is impossible for them to be prosperous. For example, consider a mother who spends her time at home taking care of her family and depending solely upon her husband's income. She might like to work but feels it would be impossible. It may seem that her husband's income is not sufficient for their needs, and he is not desirous of nor interested in trying to be more successful. Or there may be people who feel their lack of education prevents them from getting work that pays more.

If you let this thinking keep you from believing that it is possible for you to be prosperous, you have limited yourself. The truth is, it is possible for you to become prosperous regardless of present circumstances in your life that you think are obstacles. Do you believe that God can do all things? If you do, then God can make you prosperous. You may not know how, but God knows how. All God needs is for you to be open and receptive, believing and expecting.

There are two basic ways for people to seek prosperity—the human way and the spiritual way. The human way is fraught with problems, difficulties, and uncertainties. Sometimes it works and sometimes it does not work. One can never be certain that he will become prosperous the human way. What is the human way like? Essentially, it is any activity from personal will instead of spiritual direction.

The only way to prosper in the game of life is through spiritual methods. You can prosper as much as you desire and as much as you are willing. There are no limits, and you will never have to feel guilty about what you gain.

The first basic principle for winning at prosperity is to become a giver. Although I am not specifically speaking about money, it will include that if we want to win. But we can also give service. In our society, we are conditioned to become consumers—receivers. We prepare for participation in society with the idea of finding something that pays the most money for the least amount of work. Because of this, many people are in work they do not like; therefore, they cannot and do not give their best to what they are doing.

If you want to prosper, you must seek within for that which you have to give to life, and then love it and give it. Jesus expressed this principle when He said, "... *give, and it will be given to you; good measure, pressed down, shaken together, running over, will be put into your lap.*"

You may feel that you do not have much to give,

but you do. Even if you are bedfast, you can give positive thoughts and prayers to others. These are some of the most powerful things you can give, if you only believe it. If you will get into a meditative and prayerful state and ask God to show you what you can give to life to serve others in some way, you will get an answer. Follow it, by all means, even if you do not know or understand the reason for doing it.

When you have the tendency to withhold, give. It is not the easiest thing in the world to condition ourselves to become givers, for we have been trained to be receivers. We must reverse this process and concentrate on becoming givers. Instead of asking ourselves, "What can I get?" we will now ask, "What can I give?" or "What can I do?"

You have no doubt heard the expression, "You can't get something for nothing." That is true, and the opposite is even more true, "You cannot give without receiving." This applies to your time, your effort, and your money.

You may be wondering why I include money. Well, I have known a number of people who have been very generous in giving of their time and effort but not their money. Anyone who holds back from giving also holds back from receiving.

One of the best practices a person can undertake is the practice of giving a definite portion of his or her income to serve others. It is important to begin this practice when it seems you cannot afford to do it. The physically weak person does not wait until his muscles are strong before he exercises. If we wait to give until we think we can afford it, we will probably never begin.

The second principle of major importance is to realize and acknowledge God as the source of supply. It will take a little loosening up on the first principle I have discussed before we can realize and trust in Him to provide for our needs. He will provide the ideas and guidance for us which will produce the outer prosperity. When this happens, you will be involved in the human world, doing human things. The major difference is that now you will be doing them as a service to mankind and not just to make money, though you will be making money. You will not be holding back in your giving; you will not be driving fast or shady bargains trying to reap a profit.

When it seems that an outer door to your supply has closed, remember that God is the Source and He will open other doors. You will not have to fight or force others to give to you if you will trust in Him. You may lose a human inheritance, but you will never lose your spiritual heritage, which includes much more.

You can win at prosperity, for God can make a winner out of anyone who will trust in Him. Take Him as your partner, and He will help you to win at the wonderful, prosperous game called life.

What Is Your Frequency?

We hear a great deal today about "taking it easy," "one day at a time," "relax," "ease up on the pressure," and "Rome wasn't built in a day." All these statements imply that in these fast-paced times we must practice the "relaxation response" in order to find inner peace and maintain our health. This is all good advice for the physical, mental, and emotional aspects of our being. But there is one area where we really need to get "revved up," to reach a higher frequency: fine-tuning our consciousness.

We need to examine our thoughts, feelings, and beliefs to see what we are tuned to—whether we have negative, pessimistic attitudes that keep us on a low level of vibration, or whether we are positive, optimistic, and dynamic in our thinking, attitudes that lift us to a higher level. They make us feel great, like winners. The former makes us feel terrible, like losers.

Everything in life is a vibratory mass. The tree, the building, light, sound, and everything we see and feel is a series of vibrations. Things that look solid are still a conglomerate of vibrations. Sound is only vibration within a certain frequency range. The mind translates these and we say we "hear."

When we get our consciousness fine-tuned we begin to receive or become conscious of many wonderful possibilities. When the mind is clogged with a lot of negative thinking, we are not receptive to the ideas that would enable us to meet and solve the pressing problems before us. But when the mind is fine-tuned and open, we get those answers.

Each of us is similar to a radio station—we "send out" at various frequencies all the time. What we are vibrates, and others respond to those vibrations. You no doubt have had the experience of meeting someone for the first time and immediately forming an opinion about the person without much conversation. You either liked him or disliked him. You may even have felt very strong negative vibrations that warned you to be careful of having any dealings with some persons.

You have heard the expression, "He has good vibes." This is more than a figure of speech; it is literally a fact. When we are around someone who is successful we feel these strong, positive vibes and it makes us feel better. That is why we like to associate with successful people.

Some homes also have harmonious and peaceful vibrations, while others have the opposite. You vibrate, your home vibrates, everything in it vibrates. Your thoughts, feelings, and beliefs determine whether the frequency is dynamic and constructive or negative and destructive.

When we "tune in" to the finer things of life, we think beautiful thoughts of love, success, peace, health, self-discipline, self-mastery, and many other positive, dynamic thoughts. We are a wonderful harmony of success. When we are in tune with coarser concepts, we are like a young band whose members are just learning to play. We squeak and play off key, and the results are not always what we would like them to be. When a person holds the thought, "I can succeed," he is fine-tuned and thinking like a winner.

Your car sometimes is "out of tune" or in need of a "tune-up." A tune-up is simply returning something to proper order. Life's experiences after a time tend to get us out of tune; instead of thinking thoughts of success, we find ourselves in negative ruts and out of tune. It is at such times that we need to take some time to ourselves to become tuned up with some good, dynamic, positive thinking. We can do this through prayer, and we can add to that the reading of some inspirational books or listening to some uplifting talks on cassettes. A winner does this, for he knows the value of clear, clean, positive, uplifting thoughts and ideas.

Put Your Heart Into It

When we see a person attempting to perform a task with a lackadaisical attitude we say, "His heart's not in it." There seems to be no enthusiasm for the task, even if it is something important. Failure is almost guaranteed without enthusiasm. To win we must have abounding enthusiasm; we must put our hearts into the thing we are attempting to do. If we are to be happy persons, we must have a zest for living, and be eager for the encounter of daily challenges and opportunities.

Enthusiasm is the ability to have a dynamic interest in something—a goal or plan or an idea that we would like to develop and express. Some think of enthusiasm as a bubbling stream. It rushes noisily over rocks and other objects as it moves along its merry way. Sometimes our zeal does make us appear this way, but there is also the quiet type of enthusiasm, the enthusiasm of a deep river. On the surface it hardly appears to be moving, but it is; and it is moving with great power and force.

Jesus and Paul are examples of these two expressions of zeal and enthusiasm. Before his conversion, Paul was zealous for the "letter of the law." He claimed to be a "Hebrew of Hebrews," meaning that he was very meticulous and zealous in obeying the law. He was also very zealous in attempting to make others obedient to it. Jesus was the opposite—He was not disturbed when others did not accept Him or what He had to say. He had a deep inner awareness of His mission in life and a vital and dynamic enthusiasm for completing it. He knew that He would be victorious and He was.

If you are bored with life, you need to quicken the power of enthusiasm. You may think that you have nothing to get enthusiastic about. But remember that it is not "things" that make us enthusiastic, it is our attitude, our interest in someone or something that determines whether we feel enthusiastic. All we need to do is change our attitudes about ourselves and our lives. When we develop a positive self-perception we will begin to feel a surge of enthusiasm to go forth and accomplish something worthwhile or to do what we are now doing in a totally different manner.

You may be saying to yourself, "How can I be enthusiastic about myself? I don't have much talent, ability, money, or even health. How can you expect me to be enthusiastic about my messed-up life?" It is this very attitude that must be changed. Pessimistic attitudes lead to failure, and I know you are interested in winning. When you think you do not have talent and ability you just have not discovered the great potential that is within you. When you say you do not have money or that your health is not too good, you are only stating facts that can always be changed with a change of attitude. The truth about you is this: You do have great power and ability, much more than you have ever dreamed. There is no need to shortchange yourself. With right attitudes you can succeed at any

90

goal you set for yourself. Your health can be restored if you will only believe this and expect it enthusiastically. Your life may seem to be out of tune, but you have the power within you to straighten it out. With God's help anything can be accomplished.

Maybe you have thought that you could get excited about life when some things change. You do not have to wait for anything *outside* to change. You do not have to wait for others to change attitudes about you or even the way they treat you. If you want to feel this wonderful power of enthusiasm, just begin thinking this positive, dynamic thought: *I am alive, alert, awake, joyous, and enthusiastic about life.* Say it over and over many times. As you say it, attempt to put your heart into it, which means to feel what you are saying. Forget about the appearance of your life and keep repeating this idea.

The result may surprise you. You will see yourself and your life in a different way. Instead of seeing impossible situations before you, you will see opportunities for growth and success. Instead of seeing your life as a failure, you will see the winning possibilities.

Enthusiasm is a quickening power and will stimulate the life force and energies of your physical body. As you affirm the aforementioned statement, putting your heart into it, the very cells of your body will tingle with a new surge of life that will renew, revitalize, strengthen, and heal you.

As you quicken your enthusiasm for living, you will discover that, through your times of prayer and meditation, new ideas of things you can do and express will come to your conscious mind. As you accept these ideas with enthusiasm, you will find the creative capacities of your mind increasing. You will not only be able to do better work, you will be able to do more of it.

If you want to keep your enthusiasm for life at a high pitch, remember this one thing: In spite of all the problems of this world, in spite of the wars, the greed, the pollution, the killing, the bickering, the power struggles among nations and races, in spite of all the unpleasantness you may observe, life is greater than all these things! And with the help of God and the enthusiasm of man, all these unpleasant things can be changed. You will have to ignore the prophets of doom in religion, politics, and economics. If you believe their forecasts of doom and destruction, you will live in fear, and you will kill your zest for life. Many have already done this; they have the "what's the use?" attitude.

What we need today are prophets of faith, vision, and optimism. We need prophets who will inspire all people who are receptive to express the best that is in them. We need prophets of enthusiasm.

As the Mind Sees

Can you imagine what it would be like if you were a carpenter and tried to build a house without the use of a hammer? Or if you were a secretary and had to do all the correspondence without a typewriter? It would be difficult, wouldn't it?

Many people have similar problems. They try to build happy, successful lives without using the tools they have that would enable them to succeed. Or it might be they are using the tools destructively.

One of the most important tools a winner uses is his creative imagination. A person who wins consistently has learned the value of this tool and uses it wisely. If you had a good power saw, you would not go around cutting nails with it. Neither does a winner use his imagination to visualize or entertain negative thoughts and images.

Many of us have never been told how important the imagination is for living. Perhaps when you were young and told people about your dreams, someone may have said to you, "Quit daydreaming," or, "Quit building air castles in the sky," or "You have to be practical." From this you received the impression that the imagination was one of those foolish quirks of the mind that are not important and may only lead to trouble. But all the good we enjoy today in physical form was first a "dream" or "vision" in someone's imagination!

You have an imagination, and you have a good one. You use it every day of your life, but you may not be using it as effectively as you might. With your imagination you can mold and shape your life. You can dream about the things you would like to experience. You can dream about the places you would like to go, the education you would like to have, the harmonious relations with others you desire. You do not have to wait until the outer circumstances of your life indicate that some of these things are possible. It is the constructive, creative use of the imagination in visualizing these things that helps make them possible.

Many lives today are mostly the products of unconscious and negative use of the imagination. We have used this wonderful tool to picture ourselves as limited in health, wealth, achievement. As the mind sees, the outer experiences. Vision, conscious or unconscious, always precedes experience.

We would be surprised, if we would stop and think for a moment, how we let others influence us in our use of the imagination. Instead of visualizing our dreams, we visualize their negative opinions and suggestions. We visualize what they see in and about us instead of what we would like to see and experience.

The imagination is such an important faculty and plays such a powerful part in our experience that one of the Ten Commandments refers to how *not* to use it—*You shall not make for yourself a graven image.* . . . The esoteric meaning of this Commandment is that we are not to use the imagination to form negative mental images and worship them as all-powerful gods. Every image of limitation that we entertain about ourselves is a misuse of this powerful tool.

Instead of looking at our lives from the human point of view and reinforcing it with the imagination, we should see our lives as we would like them to be. See yourself doing the work you have a sincere desire to do. When you receive ideas that you feel and think are right for you, visualize these ideas in your mind. Do not put them aside thinking they are too big to accomplish. It will take big dreams to accomplish great things, so be bold and fearless. If God gave you the idea, then it must be possible to achieve.

The imagination is the "architect" of the mind. Whatever thought structures we build and believe in we will see made manifest in our lives. The purpose of this "architect" is to construct mental images and impress them upon the subconscious mind, to give it some creative plans to work on and achieve for us.

The images we feed to the subconscious should be based on intuitive guidance rather than speculation. See yourself expressing your true feelings and desires instead of something your intellect has come up with through observation. Do not rationalize, and do not visualize any form of limitation. As far as you are capable at the moment, see in your mind the perfect and complete mental picture of what you think God wants you to be in expression. He wants you to be a winner at something. So whatever it is, visualize it.

Some people are reluctant to do this because they have been told they must be practical and make a living for themselves. This is one of the most practical ways to be successful at living. If you will visualize and see yourself giving expression to your divine inner urge, you will not have to worry about making a living. You will be prospered far beyond your present conception.

Many people think that to live is to make their lives conform to society's standard of material success. Some have achieved this on a rather large scale and yet they have not "lived." If you will give expression to your divine urge, you will have all the material things you will ever need or desire and you will be *truly* living. You will be enjoying your living. A winner knows the joy and excitement of seeing his vision and his dreams made manifest.

So dream, but believe in your dreams. See yourself creatively expressing your talents and good desires. Keep your dreams to yourself. Do not subject them to the negative analysis and criticisms of others. Those negative opinions may only discourage you. Cherish your dreams and nourish them with your strong belief in them. If you will let them live in you, you will see them manifest, and you will live, literally, in them.

It will take courage to imagine yourself being successful at something that seems beyond your present ability. It will also take courage to see yourself prosperous, to think of yourself as affluent, when you may be down to your last dollar and in debt. The old visions of limitation will challenge these new, bold dreams that you seek to implant in your consciousness, but do not be deterred in your efforts. Do not resist the old vision, just calmly deny it.

Instead of entertaining negative images that limit us, we can hold the image of success. Affirm only positive suggestions to your consciousness, and do this repeatedly. Do it especially when appearances seem to suggest something negative or limiting to you. For example, you might affirm: *I am poised, positive, dynamic, confident, and successful. I see myself achieving and accomplishing my perfect ideal. I believe in God as my help in every need, and I believe in myself as a channel for the expression of God's ideas.*

There is a passage in the Bible that tells us of the importance of creative vision. It states, *Where there is no vision, the people perish. . . .* (A.V.) Vision is dependent upon inner initiative and not external appearances. A dynamic vision, accepted and believed in wholeheartedly, can change the most negative circumstances. As the mind sees, so shall it be.

A Means of Self-Expression

Your work can be a means of creative self-expression. It can be a source of satisfaction and a means of enhancing self-esteem, when it is approached with a winning attitude. There is something creative seeking expression through you, and one of the ways this something endeavors to express is by helping others, by serving their many needs.

Creativity should not be limited to the arts or the expression of some special talent or ability. It takes creativity to be a good worker. It takes creativity to continually come up with ways to improve what we do, to do more in less time, or to do what we are doing to the best of our ability. When the simple things in life are done creatively, they lead to greater blessings and opportunities for increased self-expression.

To many people, work is only a means of making money in order to live—for many it only means to exist. They find no enjoyment in what they are doing. They use their creative thought potential trying to think of ways to avoid what they might be doing. They work to live when they should be living to work.

Some have the attitude that certain work is beneath them and they will not do it. With this attitude they reduce their capacity. Another attitude that reflects the negative tendency of some is this: I'm not paid enough for what I do. They then withhold their best efforts and, in so doing, they lose. A winner would never adopt such an attitude. Another one is this: The people I work for are selfish and greedy and take me for granted. Another is: The work is too hard. When a person tries to work with any of these attitudes, he finds that time drags by; he finds no enjoyment at all in what he is doing, and he does not look for ways to enjoy it. These negative attitudes and emotions about work not only destroy our happiness but they eventually can lead to health challenges, for our attitudes affect our health.

There are winning attitudes that you can develop— if you do not already have them—which will make you feel that any work you do is a form of creative self-expression. If your present position does not enable you to express your great potential, then these winning attitudes will open the door for something more challenging and more fulfilling for you.

Be resolved that you will give your best efforts to what you are now doing. Do not withhold for any reason. Even if you think you are underpaid, give your best and more. If you do your work grudgingly, you will be unhappy. Give your best to your work, and it will be a rewarding and growing experience. When others suggest that it is foolish to give more than you are paid for, pay no heed to that defeatist philosophy. A winner always gives his best and constantly seeks to improve upon his best.

You may ask, "Why should I give my best?" The answer is simple: You give your best because you want to work with principle. Principle states: Whatever a man sows, that shall he also reap. You will always be compensated for what you do. If the compensation does not come from your employer, it will come from some other channel. Your good has to come to you when you work with a universal, divine, immutable, unchanging, and just principle. You may not see how this can work out, but that is not important right now. The important thing is to accept this principle and apply it by giving your best.

Another helpful thought: *Instead of thinking of yourself as working for someone or some company, think of yourself as working for God.* You are in reality self-employed. Your employer may think he is your boss, but you can know that God is. When you think of God in this way, you know that everything demanded of you on the job is contributing to your spiritual growth. Everything demanded of you will draw more power, talent, and ability from you. The challenges will help you develop qualities of mind and heart that you might not otherwise develop. What are some of these qualities? They are patience, tolerance, understanding, courage, selflessness, generosity, kindness, diligence, persistence, and many more.

It will take creativity of thought to help you meet and work with some of the many challenges you encounter in your work. As you look to God for guidance, He will inspire you with good, creative ideas. In expressing these ideas you will find greater joy and happiness in your work.

Some people go home and put their work completely out of their minds; or at least they attempt to do so. They may have been advised by a physician to do so because tension, frustration, and loss of sleep can result when one thinks negatively about one's work. Negative thinking about *anything* will do this. It is not the work, it is the attitude one entertains about the work.

I wonder how many prayers God gets from people asking that He help them to do their work better and more efficiently. I would wager that He gets many more prayers for a raise in pay. In the same vein, I would say that there are more prayers for help to avoid work than prayers for help in doing more work.

Whenever you have challenges to meet in your work, whether it be the boss, a co-worker, or the work itself, overcome the challenges through prayer. Do not be a complainer; be a blesser.

Some complain, "That's not my job; the other guy is supposed to do that." If this should happen with you and your work, bless the other party. He is missing an opportunity for compensation when he tries to get out of his work. Everyone is compensated justly. If you do more than is required of you, you will be blessed in some way. If you complain and argue, you will not be happy, you will not be compensated, and you will not learn a needed lesson or develop a talent or ability to a higher degree.

Another thing we should keep in mind is that all work is honorable. Eliminate the notion that certain work is "dirty" and should be left to someone else. Do your work *as unto the Lord,* and whatever you do will give you a good feeling. Whatever your work may be, try to please and satisfy others; try to make them happy through your service to them, and you will find others responding to you in a marvelous way.

If you think you are not in your right work, do the

102

things I have suggested, and you will be guided into your right work. Learn the lessons of life where you are, and you cannot help but be promoted; for God is your employer. And when you are trained and ready for something else, He will guide you into it. He is certainly looking for people willing to develop winning attitudes.

Make it a daily practice to pray for your employer's guidance and success. Also pray for your co-worker's happiness, prosperity, and success. This will set a high consciousness for the day, and you will enjoy your work and be richly prospered as you give your best to it.

How to Improve
Your Abilities

Everyone has talent and ability far beyond his present expression. Ability is not something that is just put into you without any effort on your part; it is something developed and drawn out of you. You may learn about things from others—from teachers, from your peers—but in the final analysis you really know and express your abilities because of the understanding and instruction that come from God within you. When you were struggling to understand some math formula, a teacher explained and diagramed it on a blackboard, and you finally said, "I see." The teacher did not give you that understanding; the light came from within you. The teacher was an important catalyst for the experience, but there may have been others who did not have the experience though listening to the same teacher.

I would like to make some suggestions, which I believe will be beneficial in developing your innate talents and abilities. Development of your talents will enhance your self-esteem and your enjoyment of life.

Become a goal-oriented person, if you have not already done so. Ask yourself, "What would I really love to do?" Pursue this question until you get an answer. It may be that you will have to set new goals. Most of us usually underestimate ourselves and thereby have lower expectations. Ability is developed when we set our sights higher. Talent is developed to help us achieve our more challenging goals. Raising of our vision is the first step in developing and expressing more of our talents and abilities.

Have faith to really believe you can do that which is revealed to you as a new goal. It may seem that you are incapable and inadequate at the moment. There may seem to be too much opposition, or you may think of yourself as too far behind the field. It may even seem that the field you are contemplating entering is already overcrowded. But this is never true for those who believe in themselves. Those with faith in their innate ability make their own opportunities, and no one can take them away. There is always room for success for those who have the courage to believe in themselves and who believe their goals are worthy. If you will stand firm in this faith, others will come to believe in you. Confidence and sincerity of purpose are your two greatest tools for getting others to believe in you and your ability; and, to have that type of confidence, you will have to believe in yourself.

Never refuse an opportunity to express your talent or ability, no matter how small the opportunity. Even if you do not get paid for it, remember that the experience is your compensation. Using your talent and ability in constructive ways helps to increase them. Use is a very important principle of increase, so use your talent at every opportunity. You will never know what may happen at that moment to bring forth an even greater opportunity.

Persist in spite of obstacles. Anything worth doing is worth sticking to. The person who is easily discouraged must be sure his goal is worthy and right for him. He must increase his faith in his innate ability. Get a right perspective about the obstacles before you, and you will find that they will help you in developing your abilities. Obstacles make you look into areas that may have been stumbling blocks in the achievement of your purpose. Obstacles help develop determination, which is essential in developing ability. Instead of resenting or bemoaning the fact that something seems to be against you at the moment, give thanks for the growth taking place as you persist in your purpose.

Never imitate others. You are unique. Your talent is unique. The way you express yourself will be unique if you will concentrate on being what is seeking expression through you. You can observe others and what they do, but always be yourself. When you put others' accomplishments aside, you will not feel you have to compete with them. Compete only with your own record. You have something to give that is unique and original with you.

Concentrate your effort and do not scatter yourself. By this I mean develop that quality in you that is at the moment ready for development. This does not mean you will not or cannot be successful in more than one area. It simply means that if you repress a natural, developing ability merely because you think something else will be more profitable or because you think you cannot express the natural talent, you will only frustrate yourself. Express what you are instead of what you think you ought to be.

And, finally, practice, practice, practice! Establish the habit of putting into practice your good intentions to improve your abilities.

Give with It

Having once lived in Florida, I have seen a number of hurricanes. It is quite a sight to watch a stately palm tree bend as the velocity of the wind increases. After the hurricane, the palm tree stands erect. It may have shed a few leaves, but it has survived the hurricane's fury.

As we go through life we encounter many experiences that seem like roaring hurricanes. It is important in these instances that we learn to "give with" the experiences instead of rebelling, resisting, and fighting them. Anytime we seek to make greater advances in our work or in our attempts to achieve greater goals, we are going to encounter opposition, inertia, or resistance of some type. I mean this in a positive way. Knowing this we can prepare ourselves in consciousness to meet this resistance with a positive and constructive attitude. It does not mean that we go around expecting it or looking for it in a negative way as a loser would.

According to a basic law of physics, things tend to remain at rest until they are moved by some force, and the initial movement of an object takes more energy and effort than keeping it going once it is in motion. It takes more gas to get your car moving from a complete stop than it does to keep it moving.

To live a successful life means that we seek ways to improve the quality of our living. In other words, we seek to get new experiences going for us. Each experience we encounter that seems to be in opposition to what we are seeking to accomplish can be a learning and growing experience if we give with it instead of resisting and fighting it. We can learn and progress from it instead of being defeated by it.

On the human level of existence, things never will be totally to our liking. Governments and their programs will not totally satisfy us; religious groups will not meet all our needs and expectations; people will do and say things that may offend. When these things happen, we must learn to "give with" these experiences or we will only make ourselves miserable and unhappy.

In our culture we are taught, either directly or indirectly, that to be successful in life we have to stand up for our rights, demand what is ours, and be willing to fight if necessary to achieve what we think is ours by so-called natural rights. We are led to believe that if we do not have this aggressive behavior there is something wrong with us and that people will walk all over and take advantage of us.

An individual of great wisdom whom we all admire once said, "Don't resist evil." It does not seem to be very practical advice for living in this world, but it is the most practical advice we can have. Why do you suppose Jesus said not to resist evil? Do you think it was because it was just a nice thing to do? When we understand the basic principle, we realize that we do not lose an advantage or anything else, we gain. When we consider the negative effects of resistance on us, we soon realize that this is very practical advice. One who resists what he thinks is opposing him loses his peace of mind. He also loses his ability to think clearly, and when he loses that he does foolish things that may cause even greater problems than the opposition. Mental and emotional resistance continuing over a period of time produce stress, and this can affect our health.

Now, let me ask another question, "Is it worth it?" I think not. When we learn to "give with" an experience, which simply means learning not to resist it but to meet it with a positive, constructive, and loving attitude, then we gain. We gain or maintain our peace and composure. We are also able to think clearly and constructively about the situation and discover positive ways to meet it and make it an opportunity. We maintain our health as well as many other advantages.

Please note that I am suggesting that we learn to "give with" and not "give in" of "give up" when we encounter opposition. Remember the palm tree. It keeps its roots grounded in the soil, but on the surface it "gives with" the wind. I believe Jesus was trying to communicate this dynamic idea to us when He said, *"Make friends quickly with your accuser. . . . "* He did not mean that we should accept the other person's views and ideas and give up our own. He is saying, let the other person have his own point of view while you maintain yours. Do not get upset over these opposing viewpoints. It is not important that we try to convince everyone to agree with our views. This is more than toleration. Toleration is something one does when he cannot use the force he would like to use to change another person. Jesus suggests loving understanding and non-resistance as the best means to bring about harmony, order, and peace.

It is possible to have peace of mind in this world, but not if we are filled with bitterness, hatred, or resentments. These are negative and destructive, and if entertained will only lead to failure. We can never win with these attitudes.

If we could only realize the tremendous amount of mental, emotional, and physical energy that is dissipated when we get roused up in a negative way, it might help us gain a degree of control over our reactions to negative people and situations. It is depleting to live in a constant or even a periodic state of resistance. When we stop to consider the amount of resentment some people have over things that have already happened, we can see that this is a 100 percent loss of energy. Unfortunately many people drain themselves emotionally over past experiences that they will never be able to undo or change in any way. Some people even go so far in this wasteful and destructive dissipation of energy as to expend it on people who are no longer living in this life.

A winner is one who discovers and realizes these big energy leaks and seeks to do something about them. He is a person who takes charge of his thoughts and emotions, and seeks to bring them up to a higher standard. Instead of letting himself continue out of control with resistance, he makes a conscious effort to control his emotional responses about people and events. He does not repress his potentially negative emotions, he expresses them in positive, constructive, and loving ways. A winner is one who has discovered a great secret of life, which states that to master events we must first master our thoughts about those events. He has discovered that peace in his world comes as a result of peace or harmony in his thinking about the world. He knows that if he does not master the inner storm, the turmoil of his thoughts and emotions, he will never be able to master his outer world.

Someone has said, "He who angers you conquers you." If a person can cause anger in another person, he is controlling that person to a degree. Not only is he causing him to be unhappy through this type of control, but it can also lead to negative and harmful outer actions—the person controlled may do things that he will later regret and may have to pay for in some way.

How are we to deal with those people and events that are not to our liking? The first step is through prayer or meditation. Meditation is a time of becoming still, releasing or attempting to release all argumentative thoughts we have about the outer disturbance. When we take time to become still, we become receptive to higher ideals and ways to deal with the outer negative situation. Any action you take before you do this may be the wrong action and will only stir up muddy waters. Polish things off with praise, which means to look for the good in the people and the situations.

When your car is dirty you wash it. You love it even when it is dirty because you think of its intrinsic value and not the dirt. You must learn to do the same with people. Think of their intrinsic value and not just the negative things they are doing. If you keep your mind on the limitations, you will magnify them and become increasingly upset; you will be limited by your own negative vision. If you think there is nothing good in another person this only means that you need to lift your vision, for there is something good in everyone. Mistakes do not change our basic nature. Mistakes do not make us evil or corrupt. If they did, we could never be reformed or changed. The Bible tells us that we are created in the image and likeness of God. To realize this we must look beyond the behavior of other persons.

"Giving with" means to give with thoughts and feelings of love, praise, and understanding. Most people think praise and approval mean the same thing, but they do not. Not knowing the difference, they say one is insincere when he praises something or someone who should receive disapproval. Approval is from the human level and is related to our personal likes and dislikes. Praise is on a higher level. When we praise someone we give recognition to the higher potential and we appeal to that higher potential within the person. For example, when a coach praises an aspiring athlete, he does not say that the individual is perfectly executing the desired action or play. He does praise the potential within the individual; he seeks to draw out the potential, and praise does this. A good coach does not get flustered, critical, and downgrading because of mistakes or poor performance. A good coach appeals to the greater potential, and he is able to maintain his composure and a clear mind that can consider ideas that will enable both to win.

Stepping Out in Faith

Is there something you would like to do, something you would like to have? Are you reluctant to take a step toward the achievement of that which you desire? Are you concerned that if you do not make it you will lose some security or advantage? Are you fearful that you might not succeed?

This is a perfect description of me before I got my life turned around. Among the influences that changed my life was a quote by someone I do not remember, but whose words I will never forget. Those words have made a lasting impression. That statement was this: "Many people have good aims in life, but they never pull the trigger." I had many aims, some good and some not so good, but I was not getting close to achieving any of them. I was reluctant to take what I thought would be a chance. I did not realize then that it is not chance that determines whether we are winners, it is our attitudes.

Faith is the power that enables us to achieve our goals. Without a well-developed faith, our goals are only idle dreams that excite us but never reach fulfillment. Only we can set the limits of what we want to achieve in our lives. Jesus stressed this point when He said in effect, "If you can believe, all things are possible." He did not qualify the statement by some outer condition. He knew that all outer conditions would respond and change and get in harmony with the conviction of a believer.

We often accept impossibilities and learn to live with them thinking it is psychologically healthy to do this. We do not have to do this. We can keep our faith alive by stepping out boldly in our thoughts and doing whatever we can in an outer way to help us reach our objective. It may only seem to be a blind type of faith, but that is better than no faith at all. It is certainly much better than the faith that accepts and believes in permanent limitation.

A winner believes every problem has a solution, and he expects to get that solution. He is not concerned about making mistakes. He will learn from the ones he makes, and he will not only become wiser, he will become stronger.

If you listen to the pessimistic opinions of those around you and those who are in leadership positions and are supposed to know what is going on, it is easy to get the impression that we are in for some very grim times ahead. It is unfortunate that inspired leadership is so rare, the type of leadership that would encourage us to find solutions instead of living with compromises and limitations. This great country of ours was built by men and women who had dynamic faith. They were not afraid to step out into the unknown areas of life. They assumed there were ways to accomplish a dream. They would never water down their dreams. If challenges came in the form of seemingly insolvable problems, they would just dream bigger dreams.

Faith is not something that works best when it is only lukewarm. It is a dynamic quality that makes us come alive with assurance and conviction. It may seem difficult to realize how just believing, just expressing our faith and conviction, can have an effect on the material world. According to appearances the person of faith seems to be foolish, impractical, or just crazy.

Yet, this is what we need more of in our world—men and women of faith, men and women of conviction who really mean to accomplish something good for the world and, in the process, to benefit themselves. We need people who are willing to tackle the great economic problems and do something about them. To solve these problems we are going to have to change, and this may make some uncomfortable. But remember, all improvement requires change. If we will cooperate with these changes, we will find the results far superior to anything we know now.

There are tremendous opportunities today for those individuals who are willing to step out in faith and believe in great ideas and are willing to dream and do the work necessary to express those ideas. If we accept our seeming outer limitations simply because that seems to be the easiest thing to do, we cannot step out in a dynamic new faith. C. Day Lewis, one of Britain's leading poets, has said, "Faith is the thing at the core of you, the sediment that's left when hopes and illusions are drained away. The thing for which you make any sacrifice because without it you would be nothing." With faith we can do things that will stagger the imagination. Your faith will surprise you with the wonderful things you can do and accomplish.

Faith enables us to endure hardship, tragedy, and frustration, and to bring ourselves to success and the joy and thrill of achievement. Faith enables us to use every challenge as a stepping-stone to a greater realization of the unlimited possibilities within us and the opportunities for greater happiness and success in life.

You are far more capable than you have ever dreamed. Even in those moments when you have thought how capable and wonderful you are, you are a thousand times greater. Just think, you can improve your life one thousand percent. And when you do that, you can increase that figure by another one thousand percent.

Faith is the key to unlocking your inner potential so that you can do more than you have ever done. When you step out in faith, you will discover untapped reserves of everything you need. When you first step out, it may seem that you are pushing yourself to the limit; but do not let that deceive you. If you will persevere, you will discover that the feeling was only a strengthening and stretching process preparing you to express more of your creative potential. With steadfast faith you can surpass your present limits and discover a gold mine of talent and ability that you never dreamed you had. It is there, just waiting for you to use it.

With inflation running wild the way it is today, it may seem that the opportunity for greater wealth is there for only a few. But this is not so. Even with inflation we are much better off and living higher and more refined lives than our ancestors. We enjoy things today that they did not even dream about. Put your faith in God and in yourself as an instrument through which He can work, and He will do great things

118

through you and for you.

Now let me ask you a question. What do you feel, deep down in your heart, that you should do with your life? When you attempt to answer, forget about whether it is possible. Your answer should only be based on this one premise—is it something you feel God wants you to do? If you believe it is, then that is all you need to step out in faith. If you do not have a clear perception of what you should do, then pray until you get that gem. It is faith in ideas that will transform your life.

When you decide you are going to step out in faith to achieve a new life, get ready for some exciting adventures. Your life may have been dull and uninteresting before, but, when you step out in faith, it will be a marvelous experience.

Forget the Past

In his letter to the Philippians, Paul made a beautiful statement about forgetting the past. He said, *Brethren, I do not consider that I have made it my own; but one thing I do, forgetting what lies behind and straining forward to what lies ahead, I press on toward the goal for the prize of the upward call of God in Christ Jesus.* If Paul had spent most of his time thinking about the mistakes he made in the past, the persecutions he took part in, and had let his mind dwell morbidly on these experiences, he would not have been able to press on to the great challenge before him. That challenge was learning to love and apply the idealistic teachings he had learned from Jesus.

Many people go through life trying to walk down the street backward—they have a fixation on past events. Instead of looking where they are going, they keep looking at where they have been. They keep dragging the past into the present. Since much of the past that they are dwelling on is negative, they experience guilt and frustration. A winner knows that this type of thinking is futile. There is no way that negative thinking about past misfortunes will change those experiences. Regret will not change them, and regret will not prove sincerity in the present.

Some people keep dwelling on past victories and accomplishments, but these must also be released so that the mind is free to undertake new adventures. Reliving past enjoyments in the sense that greater enjoyment cannot be experienced in the present and future can be negative. No matter how great past accomplishments have been, future accomplishments can be even greater, and the joy of accomplishment can be greater. A winner knows this, and this is why he may savor past achievements, but only briefly. Those past achievements only become stimulators for greater achievements.

Dwelling on past achievements will never bring back the thrill experienced at the time they were accomplished. Any thrill of this type will be secondhand, and what we want are firsthand *new* experiences. If we hold to past victories and live vicariously through them, this will only make us reluctant to let go emotionally so that we can go forward to wonderful new experiences. Many people waste a great deal of precious thought and emotional energy longing for their past to return. But no matter how great that past was, it is over and will never return. You cannot bring back those experiences and relive them. Even if you could go back to an old place or an old relationship, it would not be the same. Yet this is just what many people do. They try to get something out of an experience that the experience cannot give. Even the security you thought was there in the past is not there. The security that a child experiences when living with his parents would not be there if he tried to go back to that type of living. There is nothing more "dead" than the past.

If you really want a new burst of true happiness and enthusiasm for life, then make a declaration of release from the past. Affirm a statement such as this: *This one thing I do, forgetting the past and all its glories and mistakes, I go forward to a new life of success and happiness.* Set your sights on new possibilities of growth and achievement. We go where our thoughts take us. If we are thinking about things that are over, there is no place to go; and that is just the feeling so many people have. They have no meaning, purpose, or direction for their lives, and they are miserable.

In our better moments of quiet contemplation, we discover something within urging us onward and upward to new experiences. This creative feeling is God's way of telling us He has wonderful new experiences in stc·e for us. It is His way of telling us that growing and developing can be an exciting and happy adventure. He is not concerned about how many mistakes we have made or how bad those mistakes were. He holds nothing against us. We are the ones who hold things against ourselves, not God.

Everyone has made mistakes. Everyone has had failures, some very serious. Just remember this: When you think God is thinking about your mistakes, He is not. Others might be and you might be, but God is not. He is trying to get your attention with new ideas that, when accepted, will improve the quality of living. There is a glorious new life waiting for you, but you will have to let go of the negative thoughts you have about your past so that you can become receptive to this new life.

Life is simply a series of beginnings; it is never over. Even if it seems that life is over because of some tragedy, it is not. It is only over, and then only temporarily, for the one who thinks it is over. One day that individual will come alive and, instead of accepting his limited situation, he will challenge it. It is a great moment in life when a person begins to think of victories, accomplishments, and achievements while he is still in limiting circumstances. It is this type of thinking that will make him a winner, for this is the way a winner thinks. He does not wait until circumstances are favorable before he becomes an optimist. Circumstances will always fulfill our expectations if we will only expect and believe long enough and not let anything or anyone deter us from our vision.

But to have a vision, the mind must be free of the unprofitable practice of dwelling on the past. Do not waste your time on the "poor, unfortunate me" complex. You are far more fortunate than you know. Your assets always exceed your liabilities, and you always have a surplus of net worth.

Instead of feeling sorrow for yourself, feel appreciation and joy for yourself. Get excited about your potential. Make some plans for the development of that potential. Even if those plans are small ones, they are important. Accomplishment of small plans leads to accomplishment of bigger plans. Accept this and work with it.

Jesus once told a parable about a pearl of great price. He said a man discovered a valuable pearl in the market one day. He knew it was valuable, and he wanted it so badly that he sold all his possessions so he could raise the capital to purchase that pearl. Selling all that we have does not necessarily mean the selling of our goods. But we must be willing to give up our unproductive and wasteful preoccupations with things around us so that we can concentrate our energies on finding the pearl of great price within us. It is there, and it is ours for the seeking. Sell those past experiences that you thought were so important to your happiness and invest that thought energy in something new, a pearl of great price.

When we are asked to give up our preoccupation with the past, we often feel that it is a great price to pay, but it really is not. I cannot begin to tell you of the advantages of your new investment of that thought energy. There may be a sense of loss, disappointment, and even sadness when we let go of the past, but that will soon pass along with the past. Then there will be a new surge of joyous and exciting expectations of new adventures, new experiences. Along with this will come the desire to achieve, to succeed, and to win.

Do You Mean Business?

The expression "he means business" implies that a person has a determined, persevering, diligent attitude. It means that the person is willing to put aside everything that stands in the way or keeps him from doing what he considers important. It does not mean that he will run roughshod over others. It means that he will not let discouragement take hold and stymie him. He will not let others dissuade him. He will not let failures deter him. This is an essential attitude for winning.

If you are planning to accomplish something with your life, you must ask yourself if you mean business. Many times we find that we have good intentions, but we have not developed the "I mean business" attitude. This is more than a mental way of thinking; it is a strong emotional feeling as well.

This determination is essential to help us weather the obstacles that are sure to arise. This is not a pessimistic attitude. We are not going to expect obstacles; we are just going to be prepared to deal with them when and if and should they arise.

As we seek success along certain lines, there are a few questions we must ask ourselves. How we answer will determine whether we mean business. One vitally important question is this: Am I willing to put forth the necessary time, effort, and money to achieve this goal? How many times have we said to ourselves when our goal is pressing us, "I don't have time for that now. I will get started on it tomorrow"? When we make excuses like this, it means that we do not really mean business. It means that we are not sufficiently motivated to make the time, to give up some extraneous things that are just time-wasters.

Achieving a goal will take effort. Success takes effort. Winning takes effort. We have to put forth effort when we do not feel like putting forth effort. Instead of looking for reasons to avoid effort, we must look for reasons to put forth greater effort. It takes greater effort to achieve greater goals. It will take regular effort, not spasmodic effort.

It will take money to win. Another way of expressing the seriousness of purpose that I am alluding to is contained in the statement, "Put your money where your mouth is." A winner is willing to do this. He is willing to stake not only his meager savings on his idea, his goal, he is willing to stake his life on it. I am not talking about a foolish, extravagant waste of money, but the willingness to invest in education, books, or other learning experiences that will help us to achieve our goals.

This last thought leads to the next question: Am I willing to study and prepare myself to bring forth my new idea, to achieve my new goal? It is especially important that we mean business in answering this question if we are contemplating a change in our work or profession. It will take more than a superficial interest in a new field to be successful in it. Many years ago a friend and I decided to take a real estate course in order to pass the state exams to prepare ourselves for selling real estate on the side. We thought it would be a nice source of extra income while we remained secure in our regular jobs. We only worked four and a half days a week and always had weekends off, so we thought we would get rich with a sideline. Need I tell you the results? I never even took the exam. He made it and sold one or two houses, but he never made a switch from the job security he had. We were not winners with our attitudes. I was not willing to take the time to study, much less make a change from security to insecurity, a guaranteed income to an uncertain income.

To win at anything worthwhile will take the "I mean business" attitude and feeling. Few people know the joy of being consumed by the winning feeling. This comes from being consumed by a great idea, at least one that seems great to us, and letting it guide us and motivate us until we are successful. When we mean business, we will win.

It Is Never Too Late

Some people tend to feel that as one grows older his chances for becoming successful or of achieving happiness begin to diminish, or that his mental powers begin to degenerate and he must become feeble mentally and physically. That is a losing attitude that helps to bring about the very conditions one wishes to avoid.

However, you should take heart, for your chances for success actually increase with age if you will only get rid of the defeatist attitude, if you have one, and release from your thought all negative, limiting beliefs about age. To help you do this, here are the results of a survey you might find inspiring and encouraging.

After looking into the histories of 400 famous men, researchers came up with some startling facts. Of the group's greatest achievements, thirty-five percent came when the men were between sixty and seventy years old; twenty-three percent when they were between seventy and eighty; and eight percent when they were over eighty. In other words, sixty-six percent of the world's greatest work has been done by men past sixty.

From this it would seem that a person's chances for accomplishing something worthwhile should increase with age, provided of course one thinks like a winner. Right use, positive thinking, should increase with longevity. It is like a habit, the more you do it the better you become at it, if you concentrate on doing it right.

The mind is always the master of the body and affairs. This is true even when it seems to be the other way around. If one gives in and accepts limitations about himself, it is this state of consciousness that is responsible for the limitations.

Sometimes a person will sit back and say that life has passed him by and that, because he did not take advantage of past opportunities, it is too late. Opportunities are made, they do not just happen. If we think it is too late, we are closing the door to opportunity. The truth is, our chances of winning at something meaningful to us are very great. Believing it is too late only makes one weary and discouraged. Everything he tries to do is done with great effort.

It is not only someone up in years who may become a victim of this type of thinking. I remember when I was twenty-five, I thought it was too late to become successful at anything. If I had continued in that line of thought I would not be writing this now, stating that it is never too late. I still have plans for things I want to do, and I will keep right on making plans to win at something in life.

Some people think it may be too late because they have had so many failures; they think it is useless to begin again. But that is only a matter of attitude. If they would shake off that thought and begin to believe in themselves, they would find a new surge of dynamic energy and enthusiasm propelling them onward to victory.

A winner continues to hold to a winning thought

even when it seems useless to do so. It may seem a frustrating thing to do. But remember, it is even more frustrating to live without hope of improvement. Besides, who is such an authority that he can guarantee there is no hope? There is no such authority. The greatest authority I know, Jesus, says that if you can believe, all things are possible. He did not say, "If you believe *and are young,* all things are possible." There was no qualifier in His original statement.

A number of years ago I met a young girl who probably thought it was too late. She was married, had two children, and worked part time. She had started out to be a teacher, but she never finished college. I suggested that it was not too late. Before long she enrolled in college; after she graduated, she became a teacher. Then she continued her education and completed her master's degree, but she did not stop there. She earned her PhD and is now successful in her profession.

I have seen this happen in the lives of quite a number of people over the last twenty years. These people did not wait until their circumstances changed before they began thinking more positively about their lives. They took hold of the idea that it is thought that changes lives, and they began thinking about the things they wanted to accomplish. This opened the way for their success.

It will take courage to step out into new avenues of life, but you have all the courage you need within you. With an idea from God, and faith in Him to help you express that idea, and faith in yourself as a channel for the expression of that idea, you have a winning combination.

Your Marvelous Potential

There is a marvelous potential within every one of us. Jesus referred to this potential when He said, "... *the kingdom of God is in the midst of you.*" What talents, abilities, and skills we are expressing at this moment make up only a small element of this great potential. It would stagger the imagination if there were some way to visibly demonstrate and prove that this potential exists.

If I were to say to you that you have within you right now the power to manifest anything in life that you need, or any good thing that you might desire, you would probably think I am exaggerating. But I am not exaggerating; it is true. Simply because we do not or have not realized this potential does not mean that it does not exist.

Many people are unable to accept this great truth for themselves, for they are hypnotized by the negative conditioning of their past and by the influence of their peers, relatives, and other acquaintances. Many of these people live their whole lives feeling inferior, fearful, inadequate, or all three. Some even believe they are defectively created, that God left them out when he was distributing brains, or talent, or ability. But God has left no one out; everyone is gloriously created in the image and likeness of God. This is true even for those who at the moment may not have the conscious ability to think rationally.

So take heart, your potential is unlimited. Our challenge is to discover this potential and express it, to overcome the negative image we have of ourselves. As we grew to maturity, we were told some pretty negative things about ourselves. We may have been badgered by well-meaning religious leaders who tried to save us by telling us how sinful we were and by filling us with fear about a negative afterlife. Because of these negative concepts of ourselves, we have felt guilty, unworthy, and useless. If they had told us of the unlimited potential for good within us, we might have done much better, and the world might be better off.

However, the time has come for freedom. We have the greatest opportunity right now to claim our freedom from this outer harassment and to change our self-image. We will not have to fight or destroy people or institutions in order to become free; the only effort will be with our own negative thoughts and feelings about ourselves. It may be challenging to change a long-held negative and limiting self-image, but it can be done.

How do we begin to express more of our potential? First, by accepting ourselves and our situations in life with love and appreciation. Many people hate themselves because of what they think they lack or what they have done in the past. We cannot begin by feeling sorry for ourselves; that will do no good. We must begin to love and appreciate ourselves for what we are and for what we can become. No matter what our lot may be, no matter how limited our circumstances may seem, we must accept and appreciate ourselves instead of rejecting and condemning ourselves. After all, God loves and appreciates us the way we are. He does not say we have to be perfect before He will love us. He has never rejected us, even though we may have thought He has. He does not dwell on the mistakes we have made, and He certainly does not hold them against us. Others may do this, but not God. And if He does not hold things against us, we should not hold things against ourselves either.

We cannot wait until we become something before we begin to love and appreciate ourselves. These qualities should not be withheld until something is accomplished.

Helen Keller did not wait until her condition was improved before she accepted herself and her position in life. She accepted herself and began doing something to improve her life and others'. She did not condemn herself nor rebel against God and accuse Him. She may have had thoughts such as this at one time or another, but in order to make the progress she made she had to get rid of self-pity and rebelliousness and develop love and appreciation of herself. Even with her "limitations" she became more successful and was a happier person than most people with healthy bodies. Helen Keller was a winner. She thought like a winner; she believed like a winner; she persisted and put forth the necessary inner and outer effort to win, and she won.

The second important thing is to become committed to winning, to succeeding, to intensify the desire and longing to improve and achieve more than we have in the past. It is unfortunate that we often wait until we are forced to improve through tragic circumstances. It would be much better to let God take charge and move ahead right now with His help in expressing the marvelous potential He has planted within us. We never know what we can do until we try, and we never really try until we are fired up with determination.

It is not too late; it is never too late to begin to develop some quality or talent or ability. I remember a dear friend in Syracuse, New York, who never learned to swim until she was in her fifties. She and her husband owned a beautiful lakeside cottage on Otisco Lake, and she not only swam but she was diving into the cold water even in her eighties. They both loved life and enjoyed it to the fullest. They loved to have young people around them, and my wife and I and the young people from our church had many wonderful times swimming and waterskiing at their summer home on the lake.

How do we get fired up to learn, to grow, to express more of our potential? We get fired up by thinking about the things in life that we want to do and accomplish, and by thinking it is still possible to learn about these things and to do them. A winner does not give in to "it's too late" thinking. If we will think instead about the wonderful things we want to accomplish, this thinking will lead us to develop a determined inspiration that is necessary in accomplishing our goals.

We do not wait until we see the way clearly before we become interested and fired up with eagerness and enthusiasm to achieve or believe. We do not wait until we know how to do something before we become determined to do it. Columbus did not know how he was going to accomplish his goal or where the money would come from, but he was determined to do it. He did what he could, and the most important thing was to nourish the dream he held in his mind and loved in his heart. He nourished it with positive and constructive thoughts and feelings. He did not think he couldn't do it, he just assumed that he had the potential to accomplish his dream.

Some people look at a limitation and never become fired up. They think about what is against them or they think about what they lack instead of what they potentially have. A winner will look at a limitation and see it as an opportunity or a step to rise higher. We will never know what we can do until we become determined to try to express more of our great potential.

Our inner resources are unlimited, for God in us is unlimited. But it is up to us to make the effort to express our potential. No one can do it for us. God and others may help along the way, but only we can develop the necessary attitudes of mind and heart that will enable us to be successful and happy in life. God does not force us to express the potential He has given us. We cannot wait until it seems easy for us to do it. We must begin right now with the spiritual determination to do it no matter how difficult or impossible it seems.

A loser will sit back and moan and groan and complain and feel sorry for himself. He may even cry about his unfortunate lot in life. He may even think that his is the worst situation in the world. These

139

negative complaints do not do one bit of good. Oh, they may enable one to release some of his frustrations, but they will never enable him to express his marvelous potential.

Cry, if you must, but not forever. We must dry the tears and become determined to love and appreciate ourselves for what we are and for what we can become, and think and dwell on these positive things. When we do this, we will be amazed at how much of our great potential we can express.

The Best Is Yet to Be

A young man applying for a job was asked by the personnel director, "How old are you?" He replied, "Twenty-seven." He was then asked by the director, "And what do you expect to be in three years?" With all seriousness of thought he said, "Thirty."

Some people are like this young man, without any expectations. They drift along in life not knowing where they are going or whether it is possible to have any personal determination over their lives. Some even think that after a certain age life is a downhill journey. They think that the early years held the great opportunities of life and, since they did not take advantage of them, it is now too late. They believe the best things in life come early if they come at all.

You might stop right now and ask yourself: What are my expectations? What do you expect to give to life, and what do you expect life to return to you? Do you feel that the best years of your life are behind you? Do you think that the greatest and most enjoyable and rewarding experiences have already taken place? If you have thought this way or think this way now, take heart, for the truth is that, no matter how good life may have been to you already, no matter how great certain experiences have been, the best is yet to be!

It may seem impossible to surpass some of the

things you have experienced, but this is not so. John Oxenham wrote a little verse that is very appropriate: *To every man there openeth a high way and a low/And every man decideth the way his soul shall go.* The power of decision is yours. Your life, here and now, can be a hundred times better than the best you have already experienced. That may seem an overstatement, but even that is conservative.

If you want to improve your life, now is the time to begin. Do the odds seem to be against you? That makes no difference. Does your situation seem hopeless? It is not.

The first step you must take is on the inner level. You must realize and believe that you have the power to determine what you will experience. You do not have to leave your life to chance. You can plan for the good you desire. You do not have to remain sick, inefficient, poor, miserable, or in bondage. You do not have to fight the world and give in to fits of depression and discouragement.

You have probably heard the words of Henley many times: *It matters not how strait the gate,/How charged with punishments the scroll,/I am the master of my fate;/I am the Captain of my soul.* You are the captain, but have you acted with the authority of a captain, or have you let other people and events control your life? You have reserves of power and ability that far exceed your present comprehension; however, you must know it in order to use it. You must believe in this power if it is to do you any good. What good would a million dollars in your name in the bank be to you if you did not know it was there? When you know your potential, you can use it.

It makes no difference who you are or what your present age and circumstances may be. It is never too late except for those who think it is. A winner never thinks it is too late. If he did, he would in that instant become a loser. All that is necessary is for you to know that within you is the potential to accomplish anything you set your mind to accomplish. Even the most impossible ailment can be healed if we believe it can be. Many have come back from the dregs of poverty to financial independence.

If there is one thing we need today, it is men and women with the courage to think big and to expect big things to happen. There are needs that urgently demand fulfillment. There is the so-called energy crisis. There is a lot of pessimistic thinking about energy, that it is in short supply and running out and that, because of this, the quality of life is eroding. This type of thinking will never solve the problem, for it is the thinking of a loser. Our way in life is determined by what we think, and, if we accept limitation, we are bound to live by that limitation. If we assume there are limited amounts of energy, we will adjust our lives accordingly. If we close the door of expectation, we will not discover the great good that is before us. The power within us that can do marvelous and wonderful things cannot function if we are pessimistic in our outlook.

Much has been written about how powerful the mind is and how much can be accomplished. There has been more writing than doing. We now need doers, winners. In times of great challenge, men and women who will be channels for ideas come to the forefront. There will be new discoveries in cleansing our environment and new methods of personal mobility. We were not created to live and move in masses like schools of fish. We are individuals and should have individual freedom of expression.

In times of crisis it is easy to get more involved in semantic arguments about the problems than in believing there are solutions. By this I mean we can get more "problem" conscious than "solution" conscious. A winner does not think in terms of problems, he thinks in terms of solutions. He does not argue over what is wrong and fret about the difficulties, he keeps his vision high and his expectations optimistic. Sure, he has his battles with negative thoughts and emotions, but he meets these with determination. He refuses to let negative thinking get and keep him down. In fact, this tendency often urges him on with even greater determination.

Our minds must be free of the shackles of limited thought if we are to accomplish the great things that are possible. If you want to begin to receive and enjoy the best that is yet to be, you must think and expect greater things for yourself and your life. Cease complaining about your present lot; you can change it with God's help. Cease complaining about others holding you back; no one but yourself can hold you back.

Vision leads to accomplishment, and our vision should always be far ahead of our present, developed ability. Work to the best of your ability where you are, and keep your sights high. This is the way to move up in life.

Your expectations are the visions of what you one day will be. You can never ask for nor expect too much, but your asking should not be simply to *have* but to *be,* for being leads to having. Your asking should be sincere, your faith strong, and your determination to achieve persistent. When the way before you seems uncertain, when you have those moments of doubt, turn within to God and let Him renew a right spirit of joyous expectation within you. If you look down, you will go down; but if you will look up, things will change, and you will realize more fully how true it is that the best is yet to be!

Printed in the United States of America
152-F-4935-15M-8-81